Tech Detox

A Step-by-Step Guide to Mindful Living in the Digital Age

Oliver Cook

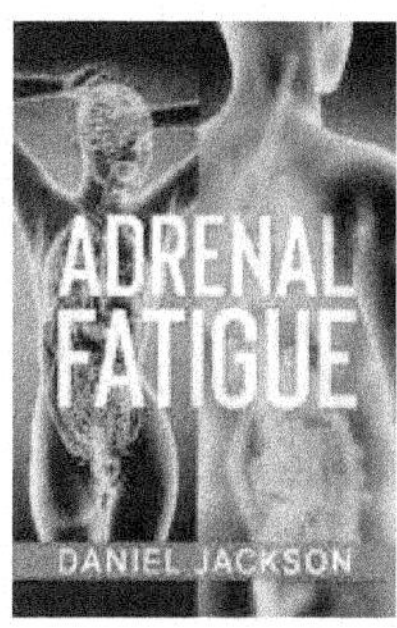

Take a look at more great books available from Rockwood Publishing

... some for FREE!

Just visit the link below:

rockwoodpublishing.co.uk

Contents

Chapter 1: The Intrusion of Digital Domination

Understanding Digital Overwhelm

We live in an era of digital domination. Smartphones, laptops, smartwatches, tablets, digital assistants - they're all interwoven into the fabric of our daily lives, often for the better. They connect us, entertain us, inform us, and make our lives easier in myriad ways. However, their incessant intrusion, the relentless beeping and buzzing, the never-ending stream of updates and notifications can result in what is now termed as 'digital overwhelm'. This first chapter, dear reader, is about understanding this new form of modern malaise.

To fully grasp the concept of digital overwhelm, it's important to start with the building blocks. Digital devices, at their core, are tools. Like any tool, they are designed to perform a function or solve a problem. Yet, as their capabilities have expanded, so too has their potential to create problems. Our digital devices, with their perpetual connectivity and accessibility, can become like chains that bind us, rendering us virtually incapable of disconnecting.

Consider the smartphone as an example. A marvelous piece of technology, it combines numerous functions in one compact, portable package. It's a phone, a camera, a

GPS, a music player, a personal organizer, an encyclopedia, and so much more. And yet, this Swiss Army knife of technology has a darker side. Every buzz, every ping, every alert is a demand for our attention, an interruption of our thoughts, a break in our concentration. It's an ever-present, ever-demanding companion that often expects more than it gives.

We find ourselves in a constant state of multitasking, trying to divide our attention between our real-world tasks and our digital obligations. This juggling act, experts warn, can be mentally exhausting. It depletes our cognitive resources, hampers our productivity, and can even increase our stress levels.

This state of mental exhaustion, this feeling of being overwhelmed by digital demands, is what we refer to as digital overwhelm. It's a relatively new phenomenon, one that has emerged as technology has become more intertwined with our everyday lives. It's the downside of the digital revolution, the shadow that accompanies the bright light of technological progress.

So, how do we recognize this digital overwhelm? Symptoms might include feelings of anxiety or irritability when separated from your digital devices, a compulsion to check notifications even when you know there's no urgency, difficulty in concentrating on tasks, or a nagging feeling of being 'always on', always reachable, always connected.

Importantly, this isn't just about the amount of time spent with digital devices. Quantity is a factor, yes, but it's also about the quality of that interaction. If the use of technology is causing stress, reducing productivity, and impacting mental well-being, then that's a sure sign of digital overwhelm, regardless of the time spent.

Digital overwhelm, like many facets of the modern world, is a complex issue. It's tied up with societal expectations, workplace demands, and personal habits. It's driven by our desire for connectivity and convenience, and by the dopamine hit that comes from every new notification or social media 'like'. It's a byproduct of the fast-paced, always-on culture that we have created.

However, understanding the nature of digital overwhelm is the first step towards combating it. By acknowledging its existence, by recognizing its signs, and by understanding its causes, we can start to take control of our digital lives. It's a journey, a process of reclaiming our time and attention from the clamor of the digital world. And it's a journey that we will undertake together, step by step, in the pages of this book.

In the upcoming chapters, we'll delve deeper into the mechanics of digital overwhelm, exploring the scientific and psychological principles that underpin it. We'll examine the effects it can have on our mental and physical health, and we'll look at how it can impact our relationships and our work-life balance.

We will take a closer look at 'nomophobia' - the fear of being without a mobile phone, which has become a widely recognized psychological condition. We'll also explore the concept of 'technostress', a term coined by psychologists to describe the stress and anxiety caused by rapidly advancing technology.

We'll uncover the reasons why our emails and social media feeds are so addictive, discussing concepts such as the 'Fear of Missing Out' (FOMO) and the 'Dopamine Loop'. We'll also take a journey into the field of neuroplasticity, discovering how our brains can adapt to (and be altered by) our digital habits.

Our exploration will not be limited to the problems, however. This book will also provide practical, actionable strategies for managing and reducing digital overwhelm. We will discuss techniques for mindful technology use, promoting a more intentional and controlled approach to our digital interactions. We'll delve into the emerging fields of digital minimalism and digital detox, providing a roadmap for those who seek to reclaim their time and attention from the demands of the digital world.

We'll provide advice on setting healthy digital boundaries, both in personal and professional life, and we'll share tips on how to cultivate a healthier relationship with our devices. We will learn to embrace the benefits of technology, without letting it rule our lives.

And above all, we'll relearn the lost art of being present - of living in the moment, free from the relentless pull of the digital world. For it's only by stepping back from the noise and distractions of our devices that we can truly connect with ourselves, with others, and with the world around us.

Indeed, understanding digital overwhelm isn't just about reducing stress or improving productivity (though these are important benefits). It's about taking back control of our lives. It's about deciding how we spend our time and attention, rather than having these precious resources constantly hijacked by the latest tweet or email. It's about living life on our own terms, not according to the whims of the notification bell.

It's a journey worth undertaking, and this first chapter is just the beginning. So, as we navigate the digital waters of the 21st century together, remember to stay mindful, stay curious, and above all, stay human in this increasingly digital world. Let's set sail on this journey to reclaim our digital sanity and serenity in the chapters to come.

Statistics: The Extent of Tech Dominance

As we delve into the reach and ramifications of tech dominance in our lives, numbers provide a compelling narrative. Statistics, when wielded correctly, can cut through the haze of subjectivity and ambiguity, giving us a clear, objective look at the landscape we're navigating.

So, let's arm ourselves with some quantitative insights as we continue our exploration of digital overwhelm.

According to a 2022 report from the Pew Research Center, 97% of adults in the United States own a smartphone, and a similar percentage is seen in many developed countries around the world. This saturation of smartphones means they are our constant companions, day and night. They are typically the first thing we reach for in the morning and the last thing we interact with at night.

But smartphone usage is just the tip of the digital iceberg. A report by eMarketer in 2023 showed that the average adult in the US spends over 13 hours each day consuming media, with digital media accounting for more than half of that time. This includes everything from streaming videos and music, to browsing social media, to reading news online.

To bring that into sharper focus, let's consider social media alone. Data from Hootsuite and We Are Social's 'Digital 2023' report reveals that the average person spends about 2 hours and 24 minutes per day on social media platforms. That's roughly one-third of their total internet time, and it translates to more than 16 hours per week, or nearly 34 full days per year. And remember, that's just social media. When you add in emails, text messages, online shopping, and all the other digital tasks, the total time spent online is considerably higher.

The Intrusion of Digital Domination

What about work? The 'State of Remote Work 2023' report from Buffer and AngelList showed that, since the start of the COVID-19 pandemic, more people are working from home than ever before, and the average workday has lengthened by nearly 49 minutes. The line between work and personal life has become blurred, with many people checking work emails and messages well beyond traditional office hours. In a world where remote work is increasingly the norm, our devices are not just gateways to our social lives but also to our professional lives.

Even children are not spared from this digital inundation. Common Sense Media's 2022 report indicated that children aged 8 to 12 in the US are spending nearly five hours per day on screens for entertainment alone — not including time spent on screens for school or homework. For teenagers, that figure jumps to nearly seven and a half hours.

These numbers, as staggering as they are, only reveal part of the story. They highlight the sheer amount of time we spend with our devices but do not delve into the psychological, emotional, and physical effects of this usage. However, they do provide a solid base for understanding the scale and extent of our interaction with technology.

Furthermore, these statistics should not be seen as an indictment of technology. These numbers are not 'bad' in and of themselves. The smartphone in your pocket, the laptop on your desk, the smartwatch on your wrist - these are not villains. They are tools. Powerful, versatile, and transformative tools. It is not their existence or use that is problematic; it's their overuse and the potential for misuse that we must guard against.

With these statistics in mind, it's clear that technology has a firm grasp on our time and attention. But remember, these devices, these platforms, these digital ecosystems - they are all creations of our own making. We have the power to shape how we interact with them, to determine the role they play in our lives. As we continue this exploration, remember: data is power. These statistics are not simply numbers; they're tools that help us understand the breadth and depth of tech dominance in our lives. They underscore the urgency of addressing digital overwhelm and provide a quantitative foundation for our collective and individual efforts towards digital balance.

Let's examine these statistics through another lens - one of potential change. Consider this: if we were to cut down our daily social media time by just 10 minutes, we could regain over 60 hours in a year. Imagine the books we could read, the walks we could take, the meaningful conversations we could have in that time. Small changes can indeed have profound impacts when magnified over days, weeks, and months.

Looking at these figures also leads us to an important realization: managing digital overwhelm is not just a personal challenge, it's a societal one. With the line between the digital world and the physical world becoming increasingly blurred, we are all part of this shared digital experience. That means that while individual action is crucial, societal shifts in how we view and interact with technology are also vital.

In the corporate world, for example, there's an emerging discussion about the 'right to disconnect' - the idea that employees should be able to disengage from work-related electronic communications outside of work hours. Some countries, like France, have even turned this concept into law. This is just one example of how we can collectively rethink our relationship with technology.

Moreover, as parents, educators, and role models, we need to be mindful of the digital habits we're passing onto younger generations. Children and teenagers are digital natives, growing up in a world where tech dominance is the norm. The statistics we have discussed indicate that they are spending a significant portion of their waking hours in front of screens. As such, fostering healthy digital habits early on is more important than ever.

In future chapters, we will discuss strategies for instilling these habits in our children and teenagers, for creating a healthier digital environment in our homes, and for promoting digital well-being in our workplaces. We will also explore the role of tech companies in all this and discuss how they can (and should) take responsibility for the digital health of their users.

In the end, remember that while these statistics might seem daunting, they should also be empowering. They serve as a reminder that we are not alone in facing these challenges. Millions of others are grappling with the same issues, and there's a growing awareness of and desire to address digital overwhelm.

As we move forward, we will build upon this understanding, drawing from a range of disciplines including psychology, neuroscience, behavioral economics, and more to develop strategies for managing digital overwhelm. So, armed with these statistics, let's continue our journey towards a more mindful and balanced digital life.

Recent Research: Effects on Physical and Mental Health

As we continue our exploration of the effects of digital domination, it's vital that we turn our attention to the latest research findings concerning its impact on physical and mental health. Over the past decade, an expanding body of research has begun to shed light on these areas, revealing a complex and multifaceted relationship between technology use and our well-being.

To provide a balanced and comprehensive overview, we will discuss both the detrimental effects as well as the potential health benefits associated with our digital habits.

Let's begin with the negative implications, as these are often the most discussed and the most concerning. Numerous studies have found associations between high levels of screen time and a range of physical health problems. These include sedentary behavior leading to obesity, musculoskeletal problems, and even potential disruption of sleep patterns due to blue light emission from screens.

A study published in "The Lancet" in 2022 found that adults who spend six or more hours of leisure time a day on screens have a higher risk of developing cardiovascular disease compared to those who spend less time. This correlation remained even after adjusting for other risk factors such as smoking, diet, and physical activity.

Research has also revealed links between excessive screen time and sleep disturbances. Exposure to the blue light emitted by screens can disrupt our body's production of melatonin, the hormone that regulates sleep. A study in the "Journal of Clinical Sleep Medicine" in 2022 found that individuals who use screens heavily in the hours before bedtime report poorer quality of sleep and increased daytime sleepiness.

On the mental health front, the picture is similarly complex. A research article in "Nature Human Behaviour" in 2023 showed a correlation between high levels of social media use and increased symptoms of anxiety and depression, particularly among adolescents. The same study noted that cyberbullying and the pressure to maintain a perfect online image can also contribute to mental health issues.

Moreover, a phenomenon termed 'technostress' – stress induced by the use of technology – has been linked to decreased productivity and job satisfaction, as well as increased anxiety levels. The 'always-on' culture prevalent in many modern workplaces means that employees often feel they cannot disconnect, leading to feelings of burnout and mental exhaustion.

However, it's important to note that the relationship between technology use and health is not entirely negative. There's also a growing body of research showing that technology, when used mindfully and in moderation, can have positive effects on both physical and mental health.

Digital tools can facilitate access to health information and services, support healthy behaviors, and connect people with healthcare providers. They can also promote social connections, provide avenues for creative expression, and give us access to resources for learning and personal growth.

Several studies have highlighted the potential of technology in the mental health domain. For instance, a review in the "Journal of Medical Internet Research" in 2023 found that digital interventions, such as online cognitive behavioral therapy (CBT), can be effective in treating conditions like depression and anxiety.

Mobile health (or 'mHealth') apps can also play a role in supporting physical health. These apps can help users monitor their health, manage chronic conditions, improve fitness, and promote healthier habits. A 2022 review in the "American Journal of Preventive Medicine" found that users of fitness tracking apps were more likely to achieve their physical activity goals compared to non-users.

In conclusion, the research paints a nuanced picture. On one hand, excessive and unregulated use of technology can have detrimental effects on both physical and mental health. On the other hand, when used mindfully and in moderation, technology can serve as a tool for promoting health and well-being.

As we move forward, it's essential to understand these nuances and to use them to inform our approach towards digital technology. Remember, the goal isn't to demonize technology or to eliminate it from our lives entirely. It's to find a balance - to harness the benefits that technology offers while minimizing its potential drawbacks.

One of the crucial lessons we can glean from the research is that intentionality matters. Passive, mindless scrolling through social media feeds is not the same as actively using technology to learn, create, or connect with loved ones. The impacts on our health and well-being can be vastly different.

We also need to be mindful of the difference between correlation and causation in these studies. While many research findings indicate a correlation between heavy technology use and various health issues, it doesn't necessarily mean that the technology use is the cause of those issues. Other factors may be involved, and in many cases, further research is needed to fully understand the complexities of these relationships.

That being said, the mounting evidence of potential health impacts cannot be ignored. It serves as a wake-up call, a call to action for each of us to reassess our digital habits and their implications on our overall well-being.

In the upcoming chapters, we'll delve into practical strategies for achieving a healthier relationship with technology. Drawing on research findings and expert advice, we'll explore tactics for mindful tech use, tips for setting digital boundaries, and strategies for digital detoxes.

From work-life balance to bedtime routines, from social media habits to digital parenting, we'll examine a wide range of topics through the lens of digital well-being. The journey towards a healthier digital life is a complex one, but armed with knowledge, awareness, and a willingness to make changes, we can navigate it successfully.

So, as we look ahead to the journey in front of us, let's carry these research findings with us. They serve as reminders of why this journey matters - because at the end of the day, our health, our well-being, and our ability to lead fulfilling, meaningful lives are what truly matter.

The Dark Side of the Screen: New Findings on Digital Addiction

As we delve deeper into the effects of technology on our lives, it's necessary to discuss an alarming phenomenon that's been gaining increased attention in recent years - digital addiction. This term refers to a compulsive need to spend time online to the point where it disrupts one's life. It's a growing concern that researchers, psychologists, and public health experts worldwide are trying to better understand and address.

Digital addiction can manifest in various forms, such as compulsive social media use, online gaming addiction, internet gambling, or even an addiction to online shopping. It's a broad term, and researchers are still working on defining its boundaries and identifying its various forms. But what's clear is that it's a real and pressing issue with far-reaching implications.

Research on digital addiction is relatively new, but a growing number of studies are shedding light on its prevalence and impacts. For instance, a study published in the "Journal of Behavioral Addictions" in 2022 estimated that around 6% of the global population struggles with some form of internet addiction.

Adolescents and young adults seem to be particularly at risk. According to a 2023 study in the "International Journal of Environmental Research and Public Health," nearly 10% of adolescents surveyed in the US reported symptoms of internet addiction, such as loss of control over internet use, withdrawal symptoms when offline, and internet use leading to conflicts or problems at school or home.

But what makes digital addiction especially concerning is its potential impacts on mental health. Studies have found associations between digital addiction and a range of mental health issues, from anxiety and depression to lower self-esteem and loneliness.

For instance, a 2023 study in the "Journal of Clinical Psychiatry" found that adolescents with symptoms of internet addiction were significantly more likely to have symptoms of depression and anxiety. The same study found that these adolescents were also more likely to report feelings of loneliness and lower self-esteem.

New findings also suggest that digital addiction can have physical health implications. A 2022 study in the "Journal of Medical Internet Research" found that individuals who displayed symptoms of digital addiction were more likely to lead sedentary lifestyles, have poor sleep quality, and experience physical discomfort related to excessive device use.

One fascinating area of research is the exploration of how digital platforms may be designed in a way that encourages addictive behaviors. Features like push notifications, likes, and auto-play videos can trigger dopamine releases in our brains - the same chemical that plays a role in other forms of addiction.

Moreover, studies have shown that certain personality traits may predispose individuals to digital addiction. These include traits like high neuroticism, low conscientiousness, and low self-esteem. However, this doesn't mean that individuals with these traits will necessarily develop a digital addiction; it's just one piece of a very complex puzzle.

The good news is that increased awareness of digital addiction and its impacts is leading to efforts to address the issue, both at the individual level and the societal level. On the personal front, techniques like digital detoxes, screen time limits, and mindfulness exercises can be beneficial.

Meanwhile, schools, workplaces, and even tech companies themselves are beginning to take steps to promote healthier digital habits. In future chapters, we'll dive deeper into these strategies and explore how you can apply them to your own life.

In the end, digital addiction serves as a stark reminder of the potential dark side of our digital lives. It underscores the importance of finding a balance, of using technology in a way that serves us rather than controls us. It's a reminder that while technology can be a powerful tool for connection, creativity, and learning, it can also, if left unchecked, become a source of distress and disconnection. As we continue our journey towards a healthier relationship with technology, it's crucial to bear this in mind. We need to navigate our digital lives with intention, awareness, and care.

Of course, it's important to remember that not all heavy technology use equates to digital addiction. Everyone's relationship with technology is unique.

What might be problematic use for one person might be perfectly healthy for another. It's not necessarily about the amount of screen time but how that screen time is affecting your life.

Digital addiction is a complex issue, and there's still a lot that we don't know. But the research so far suggests that it's a serious concern with real and significant impacts on our well-being.

It serves as a call to action - a call to reassess our digital habits, to understand the potential risks and to take steps to ensure that our digital lives are serving our overall health and well-being.

Over the next chapters, we will dive deeper into the practical strategies for maintaining a healthier relationship with technology. We will discuss different types of digital detoxes, how to set and maintain digital boundaries, tips for managing screen time, and the role of mindfulness in our digital lives.

As we explore these topics, let's remember the goal: to create a digital life that enhances our well-being, brings joy and connection, and aligns with our values and goals.

The journey towards a healthier digital life may be challenging, but it's one worth undertaking. Because at the end of the day, our health, happiness, and well-being are what truly matter.

Chapter 2: The Theory of Mindful Living

What is Mindfulness? A Primer

Mindfulness. It's a word that seems to pop up everywhere these days. From business to wellness, to education and even technology, it has become a ubiquitous term in our daily discourse. But what does it really mean? Is it just another buzzword, or is there a more profound and transformative potential lying beneath its surface?

Before we dive into the depths of mindfulness, it's crucial to acknowledge that it's not just a contemporary fad or a Silicon Valley trend. Mindfulness has deep roots in ancient wisdom, primarily drawn from Buddhist traditions, where it's called "sati." In the original Pali language, it literally means "to remember," but it's often interpreted as "maintaining awareness."

At its core, mindfulness is the ability to be fully present and engaged in the moment, free from distraction or judgment, with a soft and open mind. It's about observing your life as it unfolds, in its raw and unedited glory, without the compulsion to suppress, avoid, or otherwise manipulate what's happening. Mindfulness is about embracing reality as it is, not as we wish it to be.

Now, you might wonder why mindfulness is being discussed in a book dedicated to living in the digital age. What's the connection between these ancient practices and our hyper-connected, tech-driven world?

The fact is, our modern, high-speed life has made mindfulness more critical than ever. We live in an age of relentless distraction, where our attention is constantly being hijacked by buzzing notifications, endless streams of information, and a constant pressure to do more, be more, and have more. This "always-on" culture can lead to mental fatigue, stress, anxiety, and even burnout. It's no wonder that we often feel disconnected from our own lives, even as we're more connected to the world than ever.

In contrast, mindfulness invites us to slow down, to step back from the ceaseless rush of activity, and to tune into the rich tapestry of experiences that make up our life. It reminds us that there's more to living than merely getting through our to-do lists or catching up with our social media feeds. It encourages us to savour the taste of our morning coffee, the feel of the breeze on our skin, the laughter of a loved one - the simple, ordinary moments that often go unnoticed, yet form the essence of our existence.

At the same time, mindfulness is not about escaping from the world or rejecting technology. Quite the opposite. It's about learning to use our devices mindfully, with intention and awareness, so they serve us instead of controlling us. It's about creating a healthier relationship with our screens, where we're in the driver's seat, not our apps or notifications.

There's a growing body of scientific evidence that supports the benefits of mindfulness. Researchers from prestigious institutions such as Harvard, Stanford, and Oxford have shown that regular mindfulness practice can improve our mental and physical health, enhance our relationships, boost our productivity, and even rewire our brains for the better.

In the upcoming chapters, we'll explore how mindfulness can help us navigate the digital landscape with more grace and ease. We'll look at practical strategies and techniques for integrating mindfulness into our daily lives and using technology more intentionally. But for now, let's keep our focus on understanding the fundamentals of mindfulness, because as the old saying goes, "The best way to predict the future is to create it."

The theory of mindful living is not about moving away from technology or shunning it; it's about achieving balance. It's about understanding the difference between being "connected" and being "in contact," about choosing quality over quantity, and ultimately, about redefining our relationship with technology.

Consider a typical day in your life. How often do you find yourself multitasking, juggling multiple screens at once, or feeling compelled to respond to every notification as soon as it appears? If you're like most people, you might realize that our lives have become fragmented, our attention scattered into a thousand micro-moments. We often fall into the trap of "continuous partial attention," where we're never fully present in any given moment because we're always anticipating the next ping or buzz.

Here's where mindfulness shines a light. It offers a path to reclaim our attention, to recollect our scattered mental energies, and to bring them back to the here and now. By cultivating mindfulness, we can train our minds to remain focused and present, even amidst the incessant digital noise. We learn to resist the pull of distraction and to choose where we invest our attention.

Moreover, mindfulness teaches us to meet our experiences with acceptance and curiosity, rather than resistance or judgment. This doesn't mean we ignore problems or downplay difficulties. Instead, we learn to face our challenges with clarity and composure, giving us a better chance to resolve them effectively.

For instance, if you notice feelings of anxiety or stress while working on a demanding project, the natural tendency might be to push away these uncomfortable emotions, or to distract yourself by checking your email or social media. But the mindful approach would be to pause, to tune into your bodily sensations and emotions, and to acknowledge them with kindness. "Ah, there's stress. There's anxiety." This simple act of recognition can often soften the intensity of these feelings and create a space for more skillful responses.

This process of turning towards our experience, instead of turning away, extends to all aspects of our lives, including our interactions with technology. When we notice ourselves mindlessly scrolling through a social media feed, we can bring mindful awareness to this habit. We can observe the urge to keep scrolling, the pull of curiosity, the fear of missing out. We can recognize these patterns without getting caught up in them, and then choose to act in ways that align with our deeper values and goals.

Through mindfulness, we develop a keener understanding of how our minds work, including our habits, biases, and reactive patterns. We start to see that much of our stress and dissatisfaction comes not from the events in our lives, but from our reactions to them. And with this insight, we gain the freedom to respond to our life with more wisdom, compassion, and creativity.

In essence, mindfulness helps us move from being on autopilot to becoming conscious pilots of our lives. It encourages us to live with intention, to make conscious choices, and to align our actions with our values. It offers a tool for self-discovery, a mirror that reflects our inner world with honesty and compassion.

So, as we proceed on this journey of mindful living in the digital age, remember that it's not about achieving a perfect state of calm or getting rid of negative experiences. It's about waking up to the richness of life as it unfolds, moment by moment, both online and offline. It's about learning to navigate the digital world with a sense of balance, purpose, and playfulness.

The theory of mindful living is the roadmap for this journey. It's a guide that points us back to ourselves, back to the source of our own wisdom and well-being. And with every step, with every breath, we have the opportunity to practice mindfulness, to deepen our understanding, and to transform our relationship with technology, and ultimately, with life itself.

We'll delve deeper into the application of mindfulness in our daily routines, our work, and our relationships in this digital world. Together, we'll explore ways to integrate these practices into our lives, not as an add-on, but as an organic part of our everyday experiences. From mindful emailing and social media use, to cultivating a balanced digital diet and creating tech-free sanctuaries, we'll cover practical strategies and techniques that can be implemented right away.

Remember, this is not a race to the finish line, but a journey of continual learning and growth. We may not always get it right. We might fall back into old patterns or get swept up in the digital current from time to time. That's okay. Mindfulness is not about perfection, but about coming back, again and again, to the present moment, no matter how many times we stray.

And, while mindfulness has its roots in ancient wisdom, it's not an antiquated concept. In fact, it may just be the most important skill for the 21st century, a beacon to guide us through the digital storm. It's a tool we can all use to bring more calm, clarity, and connection to our lives, both online and off.

So, here's to a journey of mindful living in the digital age, a journey that starts right here, right now. Because, in the wise words of Jon Kabat-Zinn, a pioneer in the field of mindfulness, "wherever you go, there you are." The goal isn't to escape our digital world, but to engage with it more fully, more consciously, and with more compassion, one moment at a time.

As we close this chapter and move on to the practicalities of incorporating mindfulness into our digital lives, remember that each mindful moment is a small act of rebellion against the relentless pace of the modern world, and a step towards a more balanced, meaningful life in the digital age. This is the promise, and the transformative potential, of mindful living.

Let us embark on this journey together, and see where it takes us.

The Power of Presence: Historical Contexts of Mindful Living

Every movement, every shift in human behavior has a history, a backstory, and so does mindfulness. The beauty of mindfulness, however, lies in the universality of its teachings. While we credit much of the mindfulness philosophy to Buddhist teachings, various forms of mindfulness practices are found in diverse cultures, religions, and philosophies across the world.

The journey of mindfulness, from ancient wisdom to modern practice, is truly fascinating. Understanding its origins can provide us with a deeper appreciation of its power and relevance in our present-day, digitally-saturated lives. It underscores how the power of presence - of being here and now - is not a newfangled concept but an age-old wisdom that's more important now than ever.

Eastern Roots: Buddhism and Beyond

In the East, mindfulness is heavily tied to Buddhism, where it's considered an essential element of the path to enlightenment. The practice of sati, often translated as mindfulness, involves being acutely aware of not just what's happening in the present moment, but also the arising and passing of sensations, thoughts, and feelings.

However, the teachings of mindfulness are not exclusive to Buddhism. They're also found in Hindu philosophy, particularly within Yoga traditions. Patanjali's Yoga Sutras, dating back to around 400 CE, lays out the eightfold path of yoga, with Dharana (concentration) and Dhyana (meditation) playing pivotal roles in focusing the mind and cultivating awareness.

Taoism, another eastern philosophy, also emphasizes living in harmony with the natural flow of life, an idea encapsulated in the concept of "Wu Wei." Wu Wei doesn't mean inaction but rather action that aligns with the rhythm of life, an action that stems from being fully present and not resisting the natural course of things.

The Western Connection

In the West, the idea of mindfulness and presence can be traced back to the Stoics of ancient Greece. They believed in the practice of self-awareness, rational thinking, and living in agreement with nature. Stoics like Marcus Aurelius and Epictetus emphasized observing life objectively and maintaining mental tranquility, regardless of external circumstances.

The spiritual teachings of Christianity also hint at mindfulness-like practices. The concept of 'contemplative prayer' or 'centering prayer' in Christian mysticism involves a quieting of the mind and surrender to God's presence, aligning with the focus on the present moment and acceptance in mindfulness.

Mindfulness Meets Modern Psychology

Fast forward to the late 20th century, and mindfulness found its way into the mainstream through the field of psychology. Jon Kabat-Zinn, a molecular biologist turned mindfulness advocate, was instrumental in this shift. He established the Mindfulness-Based Stress Reduction (MBSR) program at the University of Massachusetts Medical School in 1979. MBSR was a pioneering eight-week program designed to help patients manage pain and stress through mindfulness practices.

The success of MBSR sparked interest across the scientific community. In the following years, mindfulness has been incorporated into various therapeutic approaches like Mindfulness-Based Cognitive Therapy (MBCT), Dialectical Behavioral Therapy (DBT), and Acceptance and Commitment Therapy (ACT).

Mindfulness in the Digital Age

And now, here we are in the 21st century, in the age of information and technology, discussing mindfulness in the context of our digital lives. But, as we can see from this brief journey through history, the essence of mindfulness - the power of presence - is timeless.

In fact, the core of all these teachings, from the ancient Eastern and Western philosophies to contemporary psychological therapies, is essentially the same: the cultivation of conscious presence. The ability to be wholly present, to bear witness to our inner and outer world without judgment or distraction, is the common thread that binds these diverse practices together. It is this core tenet that has allowed mindfulness to transcend cultural, temporal, and geographical boundaries, making it a universally applicable practice.

Our digital age, with its unprecedented connectivity and equally unparalleled distraction, makes the need for such a practice both necessary and urgent. Our minds, perpetually divided between different tasks, pulled and tugged by various notifications, are yearning for this return to the essence - to the power of presence.

The digital age is paradoxical. On the one hand, our devices keep us connected with the world at large. We can communicate instantly, gain access to limitless information, and manage many aspects of our lives at the touch of a screen. However, on the flip side, this hyper-connectivity often leaves us disconnected from our immediate surroundings, from our own bodies, and most importantly, from the present moment.

It's in this context that the timeless practice of mindfulness offers a fresh relevance. Just as it helped ancient practitioners find their center amidst the whirl of their circumstances, it helps us find our grounding in the tumultuous digital landscapes of our time. It allows us to connect with the essence of our experiences, without getting lost in the flurry of tweets, likes, shares, and updates.

The practice of mindfulness, of being fully present, helps us not just navigate but also enrich our digital interactions. It allows us to use technology in a way that aligns with our well-being, rather than detracts from it. It enables us to engage with our devices consciously, taking advantage of their benefits while mitigating their drawbacks.

The historical contexts of mindful living remind us that the power of presence is not an escape from the world but a deeper engagement with it. They underscore that mindfulness is not a retreat from reality, but a profound embrace of it. They tell us that mindful living isn't about shunning our devices or demonizing technology. Instead, it's about using these tools with greater awareness, intention, and balance.

From the Buddha's teachings under the Bodhi tree to the Stoics' reflections in ancient Greece, from the sacred texts of the Hindu Upanishads to the pioneering MBSR program in Massachusetts, the journey of mindfulness is an affirmation of the enduring human quest for deeper awareness, clarity, and connection. It's a testament to our capacity for conscious living, even amidst the tumult and distractions of our times.

In this digital era, as we stand on the shoulders of those who walked the path before us, we have the opportunity to carry the torch of mindful living forward. We have the chance to shape our digital culture in a way that honors our profound need for presence, connection, and awareness. This is the power, the promise, and the potential of mindful living in the digital age.

The historical contexts of mindfulness reassure us that this isn't just another trend. It's not a passing fad that will be forgotten in a few years. Instead, it's a deeply human practice that has stood the test of time, evolving and adapting to meet the needs of each era. And as we move forward, embracing the digital age with all its challenges and opportunities, mindfulness offers a beacon of light, guiding us towards a more balanced, conscious, and meaningful way of living and being.

Mindfulness and the Brain: Recent Scientific Insights

We've looked at the historical contexts of mindfulness, traced its journey from ancient philosophies to modern therapeutic applications. Now let's pivot to explore the fascinating intersection of mindfulness and neuroscience. Over the past couple of decades, a surge of research has shone a light on how mindfulness impacts our brains and, by extension, our well-being. It turns out that the practice of presence isn't just philosophically enriching; it's scientifically sound too.

Structural Changes: Brain Plasticity and Mindfulness

One of the groundbreaking discoveries in neuroscience in the past few decades has been the principle of neuroplasticity. We now know that our brains are not static entities but highly dynamic and adaptable. They can change structurally and functionally based on our experiences, a characteristic that is vital to learning and adaptation.

Remarkably, research has shown that mindfulness can catalyze such beneficial neuroplastic changes. Several studies, using techniques like magnetic resonance imaging (MRI), have found that consistent mindfulness practice can lead to increased cortical thickness or greater grey matter density in certain brain regions.

For instance, a well-known study conducted at Harvard Medical School found that individuals who underwent an 8-week Mindfulness-Based Stress Reduction (MBSR) program had increased grey matter density in the hippocampus, a region associated with learning and memory, and the temporoparietal junction, an area linked with empathy and compassion. They also found a decrease in the grey matter density of the amygdala, a region involved in stress and fear responses.

Functional Changes: The Default Mode Network and Mindfulness

Research has also revealed that mindfulness practice can impact the way different brain regions communicate with each other. One particular network that's been a subject of interest is the Default Mode Network (DMN), a network of brain regions that become active when our minds wander or when we're engaged in self-referential thinking.

While the DMN is essential and performs crucial functions, its overactivity has been associated with rumination, anxiety, and depression. Interestingly, studies have found that mindfulness practitioners show less activity in the DMN. Even when their mind starts to wander, they're better able to snap out of it, thanks to a stronger connection between the DMN and a region known as the dorsolateral prefrontal cortex, an area associated with attention and executive control. This could explain why mindfulness practitioners report less mind wandering and rumination - two significant contributors to our stress and dissatisfaction.

Mindfulness and Emotional Regulation

Neuroscientific research has also provided insights into how mindfulness helps with emotional regulation. We know that the prefrontal cortex (PFC), particularly its ventromedial part, plays a key role in regulating our emotional responses. The PFC does this by modulating the activity of the amygdala, a key player in our brain's fear circuit.

When we're under stress, the connection between the amygdala and the PFC can become weakened, leading to less effective emotion regulation. However, mindfulness training can help strengthen this connection, leading to more effective emotion regulation. This might explain why mindfulness practitioners can handle stress better and are less likely to be swept away by their emotional responses.

The Takeaway

In essence, neuroscience research paints a compelling picture of how mindfulness can shape our brains for the better. Through regular practice, we can enhance our cognitive abilities, manage our emotions more effectively, and foster a greater sense of empathy and compassion. It's a testament to the adage that when we change our minds (through practices like mindfulness), we literally change our brains.

It's also important to note that while we've made significant strides in understanding the brain's workings and how mindfulness impacts it, we're only at the beginning of this exciting journey.

Untouched Perspective: Mindfulness as an Antidote to Digital Overload

We are at a unique juncture in human history where our technological prowess has outpaced our ability to comprehend its implications fully. Today's digital landscape is characterized by a torrent of information and a relentless stream of notifications that keep us perpetually plugged into a virtual world, often at the expense of our real-world experiences and mental well-being. It's no surprise, then, that digital overload has become a hallmark of modern living.

But where does mindfulness fit into this scenario? As we've explored the origins of mindfulness and its impact on the brain, we can now appreciate how it serves as a powerful antidote to digital overload.

From Reaction to Response

One of the fundamental teachings of mindfulness is the shift from reaction to response. Typically, we react instinctively to notifications, whether it's an email alert, a news update, or a social media ping. These reactions often stem from a fear of missing out (FOMO) or an urge to stay continually connected.

Mindfulness, however, invites us to break this reactionary cycle. It encourages us to pause, breathe, and choose our response instead of mechanically reacting to digital stimuli. Instead of habitually reaching for our phones at the chime of a notification, we can choose to stay with our current task, fully present. Instead of mindlessly scrolling through social media feeds, we can opt to engage with content that genuinely serves us.

This shift from a reflexive reaction to a conscious response can have profound implications. It can free us from the shackles of digital compulsions, allowing us to navigate our online spaces mindfully and intentionally.

From Multitasking to Single-Tasking

Another cornerstone of mindfulness is the practice of single-tasking. Despite our digital world pushing us towards multitasking, science tells us that our brains aren't designed for it. Neuroscientific studies show that when we think we're multitasking, we're actually rapidly switching our attention between tasks, which can lead to cognitive fatigue and decreased productivity.

Mindfulness encourages us to go against the multitasking grain. It invites us to engage wholly with one task at a time, immersing ourselves in it. Whether it's reading a book, writing an email, or having a conversation, mindfulness helps us show up fully for each activity. This approach not only enhances our productivity but also brings a sense of calm and focus to our day-to-day life, serving as a potent antidote to digital overload.

From Mindless Consumption to Conscious Engagement

In our digital spaces, we often find ourselves consuming content mindlessly, caught in the scroll-and-refresh cycle. This mode of consumption can leave us feeling drained, anxious, and unfulfilled.

Mindfulness offers a different path: the path of conscious engagement. It calls us to be discerning about the content we consume, reminding us that not all information merits our attention. It encourages us to engage with digital content that truly aligns with our interests, values, and well-being.

This mindful approach can transform our relationship with digital content. It can turn our online experiences from ones of mindless consumption to enriching learning and genuine connection.

The Bigger Picture

In essence, mindfulness invites us to reclaim our time, attention, and mental energy from the clutches of digital overload. It reminds us that we are not passive recipients in our digital lives but active participants who can shape our digital interactions in meaningful ways.

However, it's important to remember that mindfulness isn't a magic bullet or a quick fix. It's a practice, which, by its very nature, requires practice. But every step we take in this journey - every moment we choose response over reaction, single-tasking over multitasking, conscious engagement over mindless consumption - is a step towards a more mindful digital existence.

Moreover, mindfulness allows us to create space - space to process our thoughts, to absorb our experiences, and to connect with our emotions. In the hustle and bustle of the digital age, such moments of space can be a real sanctuary. It's in these moments that we can listen to our own voices amid the digital noise, tune into our needs, and make choices that truly serve us.

Balance and Boundaries in the Digital World

Another aspect where mindfulness can play a crucial role is in setting digital boundaries. Being mindful can make us aware of our digital habits, how much time we spend on our devices, and how this affects our physical and mental health, relationships, and overall quality of life. This awareness is the first step towards change.

Practicing mindfulness might lead you to implement digital detox periods, turn off unnecessary notifications, designate tech-free zones in your home, or use technology more intentionally. It can help you strike a healthier balance between your online and offline lives and ensure that technology serves as a tool that supports your well-being rather than undermines it.

Mindfulness and Empathy in the Digital Sphere

Finally, mindfulness can enhance our digital interactions by fostering empathy. In an age where online communication can often be impersonal and even abrasive, practicing mindfulness can make us more aware of our words and the impact they may have on others. It encourages us to listen deeply in our digital communications, fostering understanding and compassion.

While the digital age presents us with unique challenges, it also provides us with unprecedented opportunities. Mindfulness, with its emphasis on presence, intentionality, and compassion, can serve as a guiding light in this uncharted terrain. It provides us with a framework to navigate our digital lives in a way that aligns with our deeper values and enhances our well-being.

In the grand scheme of things, mindfulness represents more than just an antidote to digital overload. It represents a shift in consciousness - a shift towards greater awareness, deeper connection, and more meaningful engagement, both online and offline.

Remember, the goal is not to shun technology but to use it in a way that serves us. And mindfulness, as we've explored, can be a powerful ally in this journey. With regular practice, we can cultivate a sense of balance, a touch of serenity, and a spirit of openness in our digital interactions, transforming them from sources of stress to tools of enrichment.

As we navigate the digital tides, let's remember to anchor ourselves in the present moment, to approach our digital experiences with curiosity and kindness, and to treat ourselves and others with compassion and respect. This is the essence of mindful living in the digital age. This is our untouched perspective.

Chapter 3: Realizing the Need for a Digital Detox

Recognizing the Signs of Digital Burnout

As you turn the pages of this book, you may find yourself wondering, "Do I truly need a digital detox?" It's a pertinent question, and answering it requires a level of introspection. This chapter will help you understand why a digital detox could be beneficial and guide you in recognizing the signs of digital burnout—a phenomenon more common than you may realize.

While the digital age has undeniably brought an avalanche of convenience, it has also, somewhat stealthily, ushered in a new era of stress and fatigue. The line between life and work, personal and professional, has blurred, thanks in part to our always-online devices that fit so snugly into the palm of our hands. This constant connectedness can lead to a unique form of exhaustion—digital burnout.

Understanding Digital Burnout

Before we delve into the tell-tale signs of digital burnout, let's first understand what it is. Coined in the throes of the Internet revolution, the term "digital burnout" refers to a state of chronic exhaustion, stress, and disengagement resulting from excessive and prolonged use of digital devices. It's a phenomenon that can quietly creep into your life, gradually robbing you of mental peace and physical vitality.

Recognizing the Signs

The signs of digital burnout can be subtle and easy to miss, especially because they often manifest as common day-to-day stresses. Here are a few red flags you should look out for:

Constant fatigue: Despite getting sufficient sleep, you might find yourself continually tired. This is a key indicator of digital burnout, exacerbated by the fact that electronic screens can disrupt your sleep patterns. The blue light emitted from digital devices can interfere with the production of melatonin, a hormone that regulates sleep.

Dependence on digital devices: If you find it difficult to part with your smartphone or other digital devices—even for a short while—you may be experiencing a form of digital dependency. This can lead to undue stress and anxiety when separated from these devices.

Irritability and mood swings: Constant digital connection can leave you feeling agitated and can lead to uncharacteristic mood swings. If you find yourself getting frustrated or irritable when interrupted while using a digital device, it could be a sign of burnout.

Neglected personal relationships: One of the most profound impacts of digital burnout is on our relationships. If you notice that you're investing less time in face-to-face interactions and more time engaged in digital communication, you might be suffering from digital burnout.

Lack of focus and reduced productivity: This is a paradox of the digital age. While technology was meant to boost productivity, an over-reliance on it can lead to the opposite effect. Digital burnout can make it difficult to concentrate on tasks and lead to a marked decline in productivity.

Physical discomfort or distress: Digital burnout isn't just a mental or emotional phenomenon; it can have physical manifestations too. Frequent headaches, dry, irritated eyes, and aches in your neck or back can all be signs that you're spending too much time with your digital devices.

By now, you might have identified with one or several of these signs. The important thing to remember is that recognizing the need for a digital detox is the first step towards a healthier and more balanced life. As the chapters unfold, we'll explore various strategies and approaches to implement a successful digital detox. Remember, the goal isn't to demonize technology but to foster a more mindful and sustainable relationship with it.

Prevalence and Impact of Digital Burnout

Digital burnout is more widespread than you might think. With the explosion of smartphones, tablets, and laptops, our lives have become intertwined with screens to an unprecedented degree. A recent study revealed that the average person now spends over 6 hours a day online. This level of digital immersion, while it can have its advantages, is a potential recipe for burnout.

The impact of digital burnout goes beyond just personal well-being; it has societal and organizational implications too. In the workplace, digital burnout can lead to reduced productivity, low job satisfaction, and even high turnover rates. Moreover, our educational institutions, where digital devices are increasingly used for learning and communication, are not immune to this phenomenon.

The Digital Burnout Spectrum

It's also crucial to understand that digital burnout exists on a spectrum. On one end, you may feel a mild annoyance at the incessant pings and notifications; on the other end, the fatigue might be so extreme that it interferes significantly with your daily life. It's worth noting that even mild symptoms can escalate if left unaddressed.

Just as with any other form of burnout, recognizing and acknowledging the signs is a crucial part of the solution. The adage, "prevention is better than cure," rings true here.

Taking the First Step

So, how can you confirm if your feelings of chronic exhaustion, frustration, and restlessness are a result of digital burnout?

Start by conducting a simple self-audit. Note down how much time you're spending on your digital devices each day. There are many apps available that can track this for you. Reflect on how you feel during and after these digital sessions. If you're constantly feeling drained and unproductive, it's time to consider that digital burnout may be playing a role.

Next, take a hard look at your physical health. Are you experiencing any symptoms associated with overuse of digital devices such as headaches, eye strain, or backache? These could be signs that you're spending too much time with screens.

Finally, think about your emotional state. Are you feeling more anxious, irritable, or depressed than usual? It's important to remember that our emotions are closely tied to our physical state, and long hours in front of screens can affect both.

If you've recognized the signs of digital burnout in yourself after this assessment, don't be disheartened. Acknowledging that you might need a digital detox is a powerful first step. The upcoming chapters of this book will guide you on a journey to rediscover the balance between your digital and real-world interactions and lead a more mindful life in the digital age.

Remember, a digital detox isn't about completely eliminating technology from your life. It's about setting boundaries, finding balance, and using technology in a way that enriches your life, rather than depleting your energy. The subsequent chapters will provide you with strategies and practices to do just that.

We're all navigating this digital landscape together. It's a journey, and like all journeys, there are ups and downs. But with self-awareness and purposeful action, we can learn to use technology mindfully, enhancing our lives and well-being in the process. Stay tuned as we delve deeper into the art and science of a successful digital detox.

Overcoming the Fear of Missing Out (FOMO)

As we traverse the digital landscape, there's one particularly potent challenge we must face, a concept so intrinsically tied to our modern, connected lives: The Fear of Missing Out, colloquially known as FOMO. This phenomenon is not just a trendy acronym; it's a real psychological fear that can significantly impact our mental health and overall well-being. This section will explore the genesis of FOMO, its ties to digital burnout, and most importantly, how we can overcome it.

Understanding FOMO

To deal with FOMO effectively, it's crucial first to understand what it is. At its core, FOMO is an anxiety—an apprehension that others might be having rewarding experiences from which we are absent. The rise of social media has greatly amplified this fear. As we scroll through our feeds filled with curated snapshots of others' lives—vacations, achievements, gatherings—it's easy to feel as if we're on the outside looking in.

This continual exposure to others' 'highlight reels' can breed dissatisfaction with our own lives and fuel a compulsive need to stay connected, leading us down the path to digital burnout. It's a cycle that can be tough to break.

Recognizing FOMO

Just like digital burnout, FOMO can manifest in various ways. You might find yourself obsessively checking social media platforms or feeling anxious when you haven't logged on for a while. You may even find that your mood is dictated by the number of likes or comments you receive on your posts. All these can be indicators of FOMO.

The good news? Recognizing you're in the throes of FOMO is the first step in tackling it. Awareness is half the battle, and the other half is action.

Taming the FOMO Beast

Mindful Social Media Use: The first step to overcoming FOMO is to take control of your social media usage. Set specific times for checking social media and stick to them. Avoid mindless scrolling, especially during downtime, and instead, utilize this time for activities that bring you joy or relaxation.

Reality Check: Remember that what you see on social media is often a curated, filtered version of reality. Comparing your real life to someone else's highlights is a recipe for discontent. A reality check can help you keep your expectations and perceptions in balance.

Practice Gratitude: Instead of focusing on what you're missing, try to appreciate what you have. Regularly noting down things you're grateful for can help shift your mindset and reduce feelings of FOMO. It's about acknowledging the value in your own unique experiences and journey.

Digital Detox: As we've discussed, a digital detox can be highly beneficial. By taking a break from your devices, you give yourself the space to reconnect with the world around you and engage in meaningful face-to-face interactions. It's a chance to reset and reprioritize.

Seek Fulfillment Offline: Develop hobbies and interests outside the digital world. Whether it's reading a book, practicing a sport, or simply taking a walk in nature, these activities can provide a sense of fulfillment that FOMO can't erode.

Mindfulness and Meditation: These practices can help you stay present and reduce the anxiety associated with FOMO. By focusing on the here and now, you can train your mind to resist the pull of potential experiences elsewhere.

Connect Deeply, Not Broadly: It's quality, not quantity, that matters in relationships. Foster deeper connections with fewer people rather than striving to be part of every social circle or online trend. Meaningful connections are more satisfying and can significantly reduce feelings of FOMO.

Celebrate Your Own Achievements: Take time to acknowledge your accomplishments, no matter how big or small they may seem. This will help you foster a sense of self-worth that is not dependent on comparison with others. Remember, the race is long, and in the end, it's only with yourself.

FOMO and Digital Burnout: Breaking the Cycle

It's vital to remember that FOMO and digital burnout often feed off each other. The fear of missing out can lead you to overuse digital platforms, pushing you towards burnout. And being in a state of burnout can make you more susceptible to FOMO. It's a vicious cycle—but one that can be broken.

The key to overcoming FOMO and preventing digital burnout lies in creating a healthier relationship with your digital devices and social media platforms. It's about being in control rather than being controlled. It's about understanding that you can disconnect without the world falling apart, that not every notification deserves your immediate attention, and most importantly, that your worth is not defined by likes, comments, or shares.

As we journey further into the realm of a digital detox, we'll discover more strategies and techniques for managing our digital lives mindfully. Remember, it's not about shunning technology; instead, it's about using it judiciously and in a way that adds to our lives rather than subtracts.

So take a deep breath, power down that device, and step out into the world. There's a whole lot of living to do beyond the screen, and you're not going to miss out. In fact, you might just find that the real fun begins when you log off.

The Social Media Paradox: Connected yet Isolated

We live in a world that is more connected than ever. We can chat with a friend on the other side of the globe at the touch of a button, share photos instantaneously, and engage with diverse communities at any time of day or night. Despite this, many of us are feeling more isolated than ever before. Welcome to the social media paradox: the puzzling phenomenon of being simultaneously more connected and more isolated.

Understanding the Paradox

Social media was designed to connect us, to bridge geographical gaps, and facilitate interaction. It's a tool of remarkable power and potential, but it also comes with a double edge. While it can foster connection, it can also feed isolation and loneliness.

Consider this: You're scrolling through your social media feed, viewing post after post of friends, families, and celebrities sharing snippets of their lives—moments of joy, achievements, and adventures. But as you scroll, there's an underlying sense of loneliness. This feeling, even though you're interacting with others in a digital space, is a key component of the social media paradox.

Why does this Paradox Occur?

There are several reasons why this paradox takes place:

Online vs. Offline Interaction: While online interactions can complement our social lives, they cannot replace the depth and quality of face-to-face communication. The nuances of non-verbal cues, the intimacy of shared experiences, and the emotional resonance of personal conversations—these are elements often missing from digital interactions.

Highlight Reel Effect: Social media is often a highlight reel of people's lives, showcasing their best moments and achievements. This constant exposure to the 'best' parts of others' lives can leave us feeling inadequate and lonely.

Quantity over Quality: On social media, the focus is often on the number of friends or followers rather than the quality of relationships. This pursuit of quantity can lead to shallow connections that lack emotional depth and intimacy, leading to feelings of isolation.

Cyberbullying and Trolling: The anonymity of the digital space can sometimes bring out the worst in people. Cyberbullying and trolling can lead to feelings of isolation and distress.

Navigating the Paradox

Recognizing the paradox is the first step to navigating it. Here are some strategies to help you foster a healthier relationship with social media and mitigate feelings of isolation:

Promote Quality Interactions: Instead of focusing on how many friends or followers you have, concentrate on fostering meaningful relationships. Engage in thoughtful conversations, offer support, and share experiences that extend beyond the superficial.

Limit Social Media Time: Set boundaries for your social media use. This might involve designated social media-free times during your day, or 'digital sabbaths' where you take a complete break for a day or two.

Use Social Media Purposefully: Be mindful about why you're using social media. Is it to connect with loved ones, for entertainment, or to stay informed? Use it in ways that align with your intentions and serve your well-being.

Offline Connections Matter: Make time for face-to-face or direct interactions. This could be as simple as having coffee with a friend, going for a walk, or playing a game with family. The digital world can complement, but should never replace, our offline relationships.

Remember, social media is a tool—a tool that we control, not the other way around. The next chapters will delve deeper into maintaining a healthy relationship with technology and finding the right balance between our online and offline lives.

It's about using social media to enhance our connections, not dilute them. In this way, we can fully enjoy the benefits of this digital age without falling prey to the paradox of feeling isolated even as we're connected.

By understanding the nuances of this paradox and developing strategies to navigate it, we can create a more fulfilling digital space that fosters genuine connection and reduces feelings of loneliness. It's about making technology serve us, and aligning it with our needs, values, and well-being.

In essence, while social media has the potential to isolate us, it can also act as a powerful tool for connection if used thoughtfully and purposefully. Let's not allow the virtual world to eclipse the real one.

There's a whole universe of genuine connections, shared experiences, and heartwarming moments beyond the glow of our screens. Let's use social media to facilitate, not replace, these genuine human connections.

Redefining Success in the Digital Age

In an era where likes, shares, and followers are often seen as a measure of popularity and even self-worth, it's crucial to pause and redefine what success truly means in the digital age. The reality is that our digital presence is just one facet of our complex lives, and it's essential to put it into proper perspective.

The Digital Yardstick of Success

Social media platforms, with their public display of user engagement, have inadvertently created a new yardstick for success. Likes, shares, retweets, followers—these have become digital currency, an external validation of our ideas, our creativity, and by extension, ourselves.

While these metrics can provide a sense of achievement and affirmation, it's important to understand their limitations. They measure only a narrow aspect of our lives—our digital persona—and are often influenced by factors beyond our control or even our understanding. Algorithms, trends, timing, and sheer luck all play a part in determining our digital 'success.'

It's also crucial to note that these metrics can be fleeting and are often a poor reflection of real-world impact or value. A post that receives thousands of likes doesn't necessarily have more worth than a heartfelt message sent to a single friend.

Redefining Success

In light of these challenges, how can we redefine success in the digital age? Here are a few perspectives to consider:

Internal Validation: Rather than relying on external markers like likes or followers, turn towards internal validation. This can include personal growth, learning, creativity, and other aspects that bring you joy and satisfaction.

Quality over Quantity: Instead of focusing on the number of followers or likes, value the quality of your connections and engagements. A handful of meaningful interactions can be more rewarding than hundreds of superficial ones.

Authenticity: Success should also be about being able to express your authentic self. Being genuine might not always bring the most likes, but it allows for deeper connections and personal satisfaction.

Positive Impact: Consider the positive impact you can have on others, whether it's sharing helpful information, inspiring others with your stories, or providing comfort with your words. Succcss can be measured by the difference you make in others' lives.

Digital Wellness: In the digital age, maintaining a healthy relationship with technology is a success in itself. This includes setting boundaries, taking regular digital detoxes, and using technology in a way that supports your mental and physical well-being.

Offline Achievements: Remember to value your offline achievements as much as, if not more than, your online ones. Success in personal relationships, hobbies, health, and other real-world activities is crucial for a balanced perspective.

In the end, success in the digital age is about being mindful of our online activities and aligning them with our values and real-world goals. It's about using technology as a tool to enhance our lives, not as a barometer to define our worth.

As we continue our journey into the digital age, let's strive to use these platforms to express our authentic selves, connect meaningfully with others, and contribute positively to the digital ecosystem.

In redefining success, we can navigate the digital landscape with more ease, satisfaction, and well-being, ensuring that our virtual lives enrich, rather than overshadow, our real ones.

Remember, you are more than your online persona, more than the likes, shares, or followers you garner. In the grand narrative of your life, these are but small pieces of a vast and unique mosaic.

Chapter 4: The Roadmap to Tech Detox

Crafting Your Digital Detox Plan

In the bustling digital landscape that is the 21st century, there is an often-overlooked craving that lurks within the depths of our modern existence. It's a yearning for silence, a longing for moments devoid of the perpetual hum of electronic devices.

More than ever, this insatiable digital diet has made us recognize the profound value of disconnecting, and how sometimes, to truly connect with ourselves and others, we must first disconnect from our screens. It is in this spirit that we delve into the heart of this chapter: Crafting Your Digital Detox Plan.

Let's face it, going cold turkey on technology can feel like climbing Everest without an oxygen mask; not impossible, but definitely a challenge. And it's not supposed to be easy. This is, after all, about creating a seismic shift in habits that are deeply ingrained within our daily routines. It's about weaning ourselves off the digital pacifier we've grown so accustomed to, and reconnecting with the world outside of pixels and data.

To embark on this journey, we need to create a well-crafted roadmap - a Digital Detox Plan. It will guide us step by step, giving us a sense of direction when we feel lost, a beacon of hope when we feel overwhelmed by the sirens of our screens.

Assess Your Digital Footprint

Firstly, let's conduct a thorough inventory of your digital life. This might sound daunting, but it's essential for understanding just how much technology permeates your life. Make a list of all the tech gadgets you use daily, all the social media sites you visit, the online platforms you're registered on, and how much screen time you accumulate on average per day. This will provide an unfiltered look at the scale of your digital dependence, the first step towards confronting it.

Prioritize and Categorize

Once you've assessed your digital footprint, it's time to categorize and prioritize. Divide your technology usage into three categories:

Essential Usage: These are tasks that you cannot do without, for instance, emails for work, specific software, or perhaps a family WhatsApp group that you must keep in touch with.

Non-Essential, but Beneficial Usage: This category includes things like educational apps, health and fitness trackers, or podcast platforms. They're not crucial, but they add value to your life.

Non-Essential and Non-Beneficial Usage: This is the digital chaff that we need to eliminate. Mindless scrolling on social media, playing that addictive game, binging on a show late into the night; all that adds no real value but consumes a lot of your time.

Crafting Your Personalized Detox Plan

Using these categories, you can now craft your detox plan. Start by drastically reducing or completely eliminating the third category. Remember, Rome wasn't built in a day, and neither will your tech-free life be. It's okay to start small and progress gradually.

Next, aim to moderate your usage in the second category. Set time limits for each app or platform and try to stick to them.

The first category is the trickiest. You can't eliminate these, but you can make them more efficient. Set specific timings to check emails or messages instead of being 'always available'.

Mindful Tech Usage

In addition to moderating your tech usage, it's also crucial to cultivate mindfulness about it. Before you grab your phone or open your laptop, ask yourself: "Do I really need to do this now? What value does it add to my life?" Creating this conscious filter will make you more aware of your digital habits, leading to a natural decrease in mindless scrolling and screen time.

Establish Tech-Free Zones and Times

Another effective strategy is to establish 'Tech-Free Zones' and 'Tech-Free Times' in your house. The bedroom is a prime candidate for a tech-free zone, promoting better sleep hygiene and more meaningful connections with your partner. Similarly, mealtimes can be declared as tech-free times, encouraging conversation and mindful eating.

Introducing Alternatives

A big part of successful digital detox involves finding meaningful activities to fill the void that reducing screen time will create. This is an excellent opportunity to rekindle old hobbies or discover new ones. Engage in physical activities, reconnect with nature, read physical books, start journaling or painting, or perhaps learn a musical instrument. The point is to engage in activities that involve minimal to no tech interaction.

Seek Support

Remember, you don't have to do this alone. Let your friends and family know about your digital detox plan. Invite them to join you, or at least respect your decision.

You'd be surprised how many people would be willing to join you or support you in this journey.

Regularly Re-evaluate and Adapt

Lastly, make it a point to regularly re-evaluate your detox plan. Monitor your progress, confront your challenges, and tweak your plan accordingly. Maybe you underestimated your ability to reduce social media time, or perhaps you overestimated your dependence on that news app. Your detox plan is not set in stone; it's a dynamic document that adapts to your progress and circumstances.

The Road Ahead

There you have it - a roadmap for your journey to a digital detox. It won't be easy; there will be times when you will be tempted to abandon this path, but remember why you started.

A tech detox isn't about completely eliminating technology from your life; it's about achieving a healthier balance and creating a more mindful and meaningful existence.

So, set forth on this journey with an open mind and a strong resolve, and watch as your life transforms, one digital detox step at a time.

The path ahead is not a denial of the digital, but a better understanding of when to engage and when to disconnect. It's not about nostalgia for a simpler, pre-digital age, but about finding balance in this dizzyingly complex one. And remember, as with every profound journey, the journey of digital detox is not just about the destination; it's about the path you traverse, the insights you gather, and the self you discover on the way.

The promise of this digital detox is clear skies of clarity where you're no longer encumbered by the noise of endless notifications.

The roadmap is drawn. Now, it's time to begin the journey. Buckle up, and let's start crafting your unique digital detox plan.

Important Considerations for a Successful Tech Detox

In crafting a practical and effective digital detox plan, it's essential to pay attention to several key considerations. Neglecting these could be the difference between a successful detox journey and one fraught with challenges and eventual defeat. Therefore, let's delve deeper into these crucial factors that can help pave your path to a mindful, balanced, and enriching digital life.

Understanding Your Unique Relationship with Technology

Every individual's relationship with technology is unique. Some may use technology mainly for work, while others might be deeply immersed in the social media world. Some may spend hours engrossed in gaming, while others may be consumed by the infinite scroll of news apps. Therefore, there is no one-size-fits-all digital detox plan.

Understanding the nuances of your personal tech habits is crucial for your detox journey. Recognizing these nuances will help you tailor a detox plan that suits your lifestyle and needs. It will also help you identify your digital pitfalls and focus your efforts where they are needed the most.

Setting Realistic Goals

While it's good to aim high, it's important to remain grounded in reality. Completely eliminating screen time may sound ideal, but it might not be feasible, especially in a world where work, education, and even socialization have moved online.

Instead of aiming for complete tech elimination, focus on reducing unnecessary screen time and becoming more mindful of your tech habits. Setting realistic and achievable goals will keep you motivated and prevent feelings of frustration or disappointment that could derail your detox journey.

Finding a Balance

Digital detox is about finding a balance, not about swapping digital addiction for digital aversion. Technology, when used appropriately, is a powerful tool that can enhance our lives. The trick lies in harnessing its benefits without letting it overtake our lives.

The ultimate aim of your detox journey should be to establish a healthy relationship with technology, one where you are in control, not the other way around. This balance will look different for everyone, and it's important to discover what works best for you.

Incorporating Offline Activities You Enjoy

One of the key challenges during a digital detox is figuring out what to do with the time you previously spent on digital devices. This is why it's essential to identify offline activities that you enjoy.

Investing time in hobbies, physical activity, nature, or simply being with your thoughts are excellent ways to fill your time productively. Incorporating activities that you enjoy will make the detox process less of a chore and more of an enjoyable, enriching experience.

Self-Compassion and Patience

A tech detox is not an easy task; it's a journey that requires self-compassion and patience. There will be days when you might slip up and fall back into old habits. Instead of being hard on yourself, acknowledge the slip, understand what led to it, and move on.

Recognize and celebrate small victories - they are signs of progress. The journey of digital detox is not a straight path; it's full of ups and downs. So, be patient, and remember, each step, no matter how small, takes you closer to your goal.

Consistency Over Intensity

A sudden, intense digital detox might work for some, but for most, gradual, consistent efforts yield sustainable results. Instead of drastically cutting down your screen time overnight, try reducing it bit by bit every day. Consistent efforts have a way of compounding over time, leading to significant changes before you even realize it.

Remaining Flexible

Finally, remember that your digital detox plan is not set in stone. It should be a flexible, evolving document that adapts to your changing needs and circumstances. If something doesn't work, feel free to tweak your plan. The key is to keep trying, to keep iterating, and to continue learning from your experiences.

Support Network

Embarking on a digital detox can be challenging, but you don't have to do it alone. Seek support from friends, family, or even online communities of people embarking on similar journeys. Sharing your experiences and challenges with others can provide motivation, encouragement, and useful tips. It also helps to hold you accountable and strengthens your resolve to stick to your plan.

Prioritizing Quality Over Quantity

While reducing screen time is important, it's equally critical to focus on the quality of your digital interactions. Not all screen time is created equal - mindless scrolling through social media is vastly different from learning a new skill through an online course or having a heartfelt video call with a loved one. Prioritize meaningful and productive digital activities over passive and unfulfilling ones.

Mindfulness Practice

Integrating mindfulness practices into your daily routine can significantly enhance your digital detox efforts. Techniques such as meditation, deep-breathing exercises, or simply cultivating awareness of your thoughts and actions can help you resist digital distractions, understand your tech habits better, and stay focused on your detox goals.

Planning for Post-Detox Digital Life

Finally, it's essential to consider how you will maintain a balanced digital life after your detox period ends. This might involve setting rules for tech usage, continuing with tech-free times and zones, or making a conscious effort to engage in offline activities regularly. A successful digital detox is not just about taking a break from technology; it's about forging a healthier, more balanced, and more mindful relationship with technology in the long run.

Digital detox is not an end in itself; it's a means to an end - the end being a life where you can enjoy the benefits of technology without letting it control your time, your attention, and your life.

Remember, the journey towards digital detoxification is deeply personal, and it's about progress, not perfection. Stay patient, stay resilient, and most importantly, stay committed to your digital well-being. The road to a balanced digital life is full of discoveries and transformations. Enjoy the journey!

The Art of Slow Living: Embracing Boredom

As our lives become increasingly digital, our attention is perpetually split between multiple screens, alerts, and notifications. This constant bombardment of information has created an environment where moments of quiet, of pause, of simply doing nothing, seem alien to us. We have, in essence, lost the ability to be bored. But here's a radical idea: what if we could reclaim boredom? What if, instead of running from it, we embraced it?

Welcome to the art of slow living, a philosophy that encourages us to decelerate, to disconnect from the digital, and reconnect with our own selves, our environment, and the people around us. At the heart of slow living lies the reclamation of boredom - not as a negative state to be avoided, but as a space for creativity, reflection, and conscious living.

Reframing Boredom

Traditionally, boredom has been perceived negatively, a state of emptiness or idleness that we need to fill up with something - anything. However, the constant stimulation provided by digital technologies is rarely fulfilling. In fact, it often leaves us feeling more drained and restless. On the other hand, boredom can be seen as an opportunity for us to switch off from the external noise and tune into our inner selves.

Boredom as a Catalyst for Creativity

Contrary to popular belief, boredom can actually be a catalyst for creativity. When we're bored, our minds, instead of being focused on the outside world, start exploring the inner world of our thoughts and imaginations. This inward journey can spark creative insights and lead to problem-solving, making boredom a potential source of creativity and innovation.

The Art of Doing Nothing

In our go-go-go world, the idea of doing nothing can seem daunting, even wasteful. But doing nothing doesn't mean idling away aimlessly. It means stepping away from purposeful tasks and letting our minds wander. It means staring out of a window, watching the sunset, or simply sitting with our thoughts.

This practice of doing nothing, also known as 'Niksen' in Dutch culture, is a core aspect of slow living. It promotes relaxation, reduces stress, and cultivates mindfulness. So the next time you find a few spare moments, instead of reaching out for your phone, try doing nothing. You might be surprised by how rejuvenating it can be.

Practicing Mindfulness

The practice of mindfulness is key to embracing boredom. Mindfulness is about living in the present, being fully aware of your thoughts, feelings, and environment without judging or reacting. When we're mindful, we can appreciate the small, ordinary moments of life that we often overlook. It allows us to savour the process of slowing down, of embracing boredom, and of living consciously.

Reconnecting with Nature

One of the most effective ways of embracing slow living and boredom is to reconnect with nature. Nature operates on its own time - it doesn't rush, yet everything gets done. Spending time in nature, be it hiking, gardening, or simply sitting in a park, can help us sync with this natural rhythm, promoting relaxation and a sense of peace.

The Value of Real-world Connections

In the age of digital communications, we often forget the value of face-to-face interactions. Real-world connections, whether it's a deep conversation with a friend, a family dinner without digital distractions, or a community event, offer a richness of experience that virtual interactions often lack. By opting for these real-world connections, we can nourish our social wellbeing, enhance our sense of community, and reclaim the joy of slow, meaningful interactions.

Embracing boredom and the art of slow living is not about shunning technology or halting productivity. Rather, it's about restoring balance. It's about recognizing that constant stimulation and busyness are not prerequisites for a fulfilling life. It's about allowing ourselves the space to breathe, to reflect, and to connect deeply with ourselves and the world around us.

Slow living is about savouring the journey, not just rushing towards the destination. It's about embracing the quiet, the still, and yes, the boring. It's about understanding that in those moments of 'doing nothing,' we might actually be opening up a space for something beautiful to emerge.

So, dare to be bored. Dare to disconnect. Dare to slow down. In this seemingly uneventful space, you may just find the peace, clarity, and creativity you've been seeking. In the humdrum and the mundane, you might discover the extraordinary. In the boredom, you might unearth a treasure trove of self-awareness and inspiration.

After all, as renowned poet and philosopher Henry David Thoreau once said, "It's not what you look at that matters. It's what you see." Maybe it's time we looked at boredom differently and appreciated it for what it truly is - a door to conscious, mindful, and soulful living. So, go on, unlock the door, embrace boredom, and welcome to the art of slow living!

Beyond the Screen: Rekindling Real-world Interactions

In our tech-saturated world, where our social life often exists within the confines of screens, there is a growing yearning for real-world interactions. As we immerse ourselves in the art of slow living, it becomes essential to shift our focus from virtual communication to fostering meaningful, in-person connections. But how exactly do we rekindle these real-world interactions in a world that's rapidly digitizing? Let's explore.

The Power of Presence

Physical presence offers a richness that virtual communication often lacks. It encompasses not just words but also tone of voice, facial expressions, gestures, and even silence. This plethora of non-verbal cues adds depth to our communications, making them more meaningful and satisfying.

Make it a point to invest in face-to-face interactions, be it having a coffee with a friend, a picnic with family, or a casual chat with a colleague in the office. These interactions allow us to truly connect with others, fostering a sense of belonging and community.

Connecting through Shared Experiences

Shared experiences are a powerful way of forging strong bonds. This could be anything from participating in a community project, attending a concert or a festival, or engaging in a group hobby.

Such experiences not only provide opportunities for meaningful interactions but also create shared memories, a sense of camaraderie, and a deeper connection. Plus, they often involve fun and laughter, which are excellent stress-busters!

The Joy of Letter Writing

In our digital age, the art of letter writing has become a rare practice. However, writing a letter to a loved one can be a deeply personal and thoughtful way of expressing your feelings. It requires time and effort, which in itself speaks volumes about your regard for the person.

Receiving a handwritten letter can be an incredibly heartwarming experience. It's a physical reminder of someone's affection for you, something you can hold, keep, and cherish. So, why not pick up a pen and write a letter to someone you care about?

Volunteering and Community Involvement

Getting involved in local community activities or volunteering for a cause you believe in can lead to meaningful real-world interactions. Such activities allow you to connect with like-minded individuals, contribute positively to your community, and gain a sense of purpose and fulfillment.

The Importance of Quality Time

In our fast-paced world, it's easy to forget the importance of spending quality time with our loved ones. Make it a point to carve out uninterrupted time for your family and friends. This could be a mealtime where everyone is present, a weekly game night, or a regular family outing.

Remember, it's not just about the quantity of time but the quality. Make sure these are times when everyone is fully present, with no screens to distract from the interaction.

Mindful Listening

Often, in our conversations, we're so focused on what we're going to say next that we fail to truly listen to the other person. Mindful listening involves being fully present and giving your undivided attention to the speaker. It's about understanding their perspective, empathizing with them, and responding thoughtfully. Practicing mindful listening can greatly enhance the quality of our real-world interactions.

Embracing Spontaneity

Not all real-world interactions need to be planned. Sometimes, the most memorable interactions are those that happen spontaneously - a chance meeting with a friend in a bookstore, a heart-to-heart conversation with a stranger on a train, or a random act of kindness for someone in need.

Embrace these spontaneous interactions. They can add an element of surprise and delight to your life, making it richer and more interesting.

Rekindling real-world interactions is not just about reducing screen time; it's about enriching our lives with deeper, more meaningful connections. It's about valuing the power of touch, of shared experiences, of mutual presence. It's about recognizing that there's a world beyond the screens that's vibrant, real, and incredibly fulfilling.

Furthermore, fostering these real-world connections does not mean you have to shun technology completely. Instead, use it as a tool to facilitate these connections - plan a meet-up, find local community events, or discover shared hobbies. However, ensure that technology serves as a bridge to these connections, not a barrier.

The pandemic has taught us a valuable lesson - that despite the convenience of technology, we crave real, human connections. We miss the warmth of a hug, the joy of shared laughter, the comfort of a shared silence. As we navigate our way through this digital age, let's ensure we hold on to these invaluable, irreplaceable human connections.

As you journey on this path of digital detox and slow living, remember to look up from your screens and engage with the world around you. Share a smile, start a conversation, lend a hand.

Real-world interactions are waiting for you at every corner. It's time to step out and embrace them. Because in the end, we're not just human beings; we're human 'connectings.' Let's cherish and nurture these connections, for they are the essence of our humanity.

Chapter 5: Integrating Mindfulness in Your Tech Detox Journey

Mindfulness Techniques for Reducing Digital Dependency

Welcome to Chapter 5, where we venture into the world of mindfulness and its transformative potential to reduce digital dependency. In our increasingly connected world, where the screens of smartphones, tablets, and laptops are a ubiquitous presence, it can be difficult to envision a lifestyle less dominated by digital devices.

However, mindfulness, an ancient practice rooted in Buddhist tradition but today widely recognized and incorporated into modern psychology, can play a pivotal role in achieving balance in our digital lives.

First things first, let's define mindfulness. In essence, mindfulness is the practice of purposefully focusing your attention on the present moment—and accepting it without judgment. This doesn't mean ignoring our thoughts, feelings, or the world around us. It is about observing them, understanding them, and learning not to get swept away with them.

Now, how can mindfulness play a role in our tech detox journey? Let's dive into it.

1. Mindfulness and Awareness

A key principle of mindfulness is the cultivation of awareness—awareness of our thoughts, emotions, physical sensations, and environment. In the context of digital dependency, this involves becoming aware of our tech usage habits. How often do we check our phones? Do we reflexively open social media apps when we're bored or anxious? Do we reach for our devices the moment we wake up?

By cultivating awareness, we start to understand our digital habits better, and with that understanding, we can begin to change them. Start noting down your tech usage patterns, your emotional states before, during, and after the usage. This self-awareness forms the first step of mindfulness-based tech detox.

2. Mindful Tech Usage

Once we become aware of our digital habits, the next step is to introduce mindfulness into the act of using technology itself. This means being fully present and aware when interacting with our devices. Instead of mindlessly scrolling through social media feeds or multitasking between different apps, we start to use our devices with purpose and intention.

Before picking up your device, ask yourself, "What is my intention behind this usage?" Are you expecting an important email, or are you simply bored? By being mindful, you make your digital interaction a conscious choice rather than an automatic habit.

3. Mindful Breaks

Our daily lives often run at a frenetic pace, and our digital devices are frequently a contributor to that sense of continuous hustle. Incorporating mindful breaks into your day can help restore balance.

A mindful break could involve a few minutes of focused breathing, a short walk in nature without your phone, or simply sitting quietly with a cup of tea. These breaks provide a counterbalance to the constant stream of digital input, giving your mind the space to relax and reset.

4. Digital Mindfulness Apps

Ironically, technology itself can aid in our mindful tech detox journey. Numerous mindfulness and meditation apps, such as Headspace and Calm, offer guided practices to cultivate mindfulness. But remember, the goal is not to substitute one form of digital dependency for another. These tools should be used sparingly and purposefully, not as another source of endless scrolling.

5. Mindful Communication

Digital communication often lacks the depth and emotional nuances of face-to-face conversation. Yet, we can introduce mindfulness here as well. Before sending a message or email, take a moment to pause. Reflect on your words—are they kind? Necessary? True? This practice of mindful communication can enhance our digital interactions, making them more meaningful and less compulsive.

6. Mindful Environment

It's not just our devices; our physical environment significantly influences our tech usage. A cluttered workspace with scattered gadgets can subconsciously promote digital dependency. Mindfully arranging your environment, creating specific zones for tech and tech-free activities, can have a powerful impact. Designate areas in your home for mindful, non-digital activities such as reading, painting, or yoga.

7. Setting Mindful Boundaries

In your tech detox journey, setting boundaries is paramount. Deciding when to use and when not to use your devices can be a mindful practice in itself. For instance, you could create a rule of no devices at the dinner table or turning off digital devices an hour before sleep. This is not a form of self-punishment, but rather an act of self-care, recognizing that your well-being is more important than any email or notification.

8. The Practice of Gratitude

Gratitude is a powerful component of mindfulness. Taking time each day to appreciate life outside the digital realm can provide a fresh perspective. You could maintain a gratitude journal, writing down things you are thankful for each day that are not related to technology. This helps reinforce the pleasures and benefits of a life less dependent on digital devices.

9. Mindful Exercise

Physical activity is known to have countless benefits for mental health. Incorporating exercise into your tech detox can improve your mood and reduce feelings of withdrawal that may come with reducing screen time. Mindful exercise, such as yoga or tai chi, can help maintain focus on the present moment and away from the buzz of technology.

10. Mindfulness Meditation

Lastly, a regular mindfulness meditation practice can greatly support your tech detox. Taking time each day to sit quietly and focus on your breath, allowing thoughts and feelings to arise without judgment, can offer a sense of peace and calm in contrast to the digital noise. Meditation not only reduces stress but also helps cultivate the skills of focus and attention, which can be particularly beneficial in resisting digital distractions.

Remember, mindfulness is not a quick fix. It's a lifelong practice that deepens with time. In the context of a tech detox, mindfulness doesn't mean we never use digital devices; instead, we learn to use them in a way that supports, rather than undermines, our well-being.

By introducing these mindfulness techniques into your routine, you'll be well on your way to a more balanced, healthier digital life.

Mindful Breaks: Micro-Detox in a Busy Day

We've all been there, trapped in a seemingly unending cycle of digital demands: emails pouring in, notifications pinging, video meetings stacked back-to-back. The boundaries between work and rest blur as screens pervade every corner of our lives. Yet, amidst this digital frenzy, the concept of "mindful breaks" can serve as an oasis of calm— a micro-detox that allows you to press pause, reconnect with the present moment, and recharge your mental batteries.

But what exactly are mindful breaks? And more importantly, how can you weave them into your busy day? Let's delve into that.

What Are Mindful Breaks?

Mindful breaks, as the term suggests, are intentional pauses in your day when you set aside your digital devices and engage in an activity that brings you fully into the present moment. The objective is to disconnect from the digital sphere, reduce cognitive overload, and refocus your attention on the here and now.

Unlike regular breaks, where you might shift from one form of screen to another—from a work laptop to a smartphone, perhaps—a mindful break is about creating a clear digital divide. You intentionally move away from screens and immerse yourself in a non-digital activity that demands your full attention and presence.

The Importance of Mindful Breaks

Before we explore how to incorporate mindful breaks into your day, let's consider why they're worth your time. The continuous influx of digital information can leave us feeling mentally exhausted, reducing our ability to concentrate, make decisions, and manage stress effectively. These micro-detox moments can help to:

Reset your mind: Mindful breaks provide a much-needed respite for your brain, allowing it to rest and recharge. This can enhance cognitive functions like memory, attention, and problem-solving.

Reduce stress: By focusing on the present moment, you quieten the mind and slow the pace, which can significantly reduce stress levels.

Improve mood: Engaging in mindful activities that you enjoy can boost your mood and overall sense of well-being.

Enhance productivity: Despite taking time away from your tasks, mindful breaks can paradoxically increase productivity. By allowing your mind to rest and rejuvenate, you're more focused and efficient when you return to work.

Incorporating Mindful Breaks into Your Day

Now, let's consider how to incorporate these potent pauses into your daily routine. Remember, the goal here isn't to add another task to your to-do list but to create small pockets of mindful calm throughout your day.

Schedule them: Treat mindful breaks as appointments with yourself. Set reminders, if necessary, until they become a habitual part of your day.

Start small: Your mindful breaks don't need to be lengthy. Even a few minutes can be beneficial. Over time, as you become more comfortable with the practice, you can gradually extend the duration.

Choose mindful activities you enjoy: This could be anything that brings you fully into the present moment. It could be a short walk, a quick meditation session, a few minutes of deep breathing, or simply enjoying a cup of tea. The key is to choose an activity that resonates with you and doesn't feel like a chore.

Make it a digital-free zone: The essence of a mindful break is to step away from digital devices. Turn off notifications, or better yet, leave your devices in a different room.

Be fully present: During your mindful break, engage all your senses. If you're having a cup of tea, for example, feel the warmth of the cup in your hand, smell the aroma, taste the flavors. Fully immerse yourself in the experience and let it anchor you to the present moment.

Mindful Breaks in Practice

Now, let's look at a few practical examples of mindful breaks that you can easily incorporate into your daily routine:

Deep Breathing: A simple yet effective practice that you can do almost anywhere. Close your eyes, take a deep breath in, hold for a few seconds, and then exhale slowly. Repeat this several times, focusing your attention solely on your breath.

Walking Meditation: This involves fully focusing on the experience of walking: the sensation of your feet touching the ground, the rhythm of your breath, the movement of your arms, the sounds around you.

Mindful Eating: Instead of mindlessly consuming a meal while staring at a screen, try to eat mindfully, savoring each bite, appreciating the taste, texture, and aroma of your food.

Stretching: Take a few minutes to stretch your body, paying attention to the sensations in each muscle group as you do so.

Nature Break: If possible, spend a few minutes outside. Notice the colors, sounds, and smells around you. Even tending to a small plant indoors can offer a similar moment of connection with nature.

Journaling: Write down your thoughts or feelings in a journal. This can help to clear your mind and bring you back to the present moment.

Gratitude Reflection: Reflect on something you're grateful for. This can shift your focus from digital stressors to positive aspects of your life.

The key to a successful mindful break is not what you do, but how you do it—with full presence and attention. Whether it's two minutes or twenty, these mindful breaks can serve as stepping stones in your journey towards digital detoxification and healthier tech habits. They remind us that we're more than our digital selves, capable of experiencing rich, meaningful moments outside the realm of screens.

As you navigate your day, remember to pause, breathe, and reconnect with the now. After all, life isn't happening in the emails, the social media posts, or the video calls. It's happening here, in this very moment—the one you're living right now. So give yourself the gift of experiencing it fully. In doing so, you'll not only reduce your digital dependency but also enhance your overall well-being, one mindful break at a time.

So, as you continue to read, remember to take your mindful breaks, to pause and breathe, and to let the present moment be enough.

Mindful Notifications: A New Approach to Tech Interruptions

We live in an era of perpetual digital interruption. Our day begins with the ping of an alarm on our smartphone, followed by a cascade of notifications—emails, text messages, social media updates, news alerts, and more. These ceaseless tech interruptions can leave us feeling overwhelmed, anxious, and perpetually distracted. In this section, we'll explore a new approach to manage these digital disturbances, one rooted in mindfulness: mindful notifications.

Understanding the Impact of Notifications

Before we delve into mindful notifications, it's important to understand why traditional notifications can be so disruptive.

Each time we hear a notification, our attention is involuntarily pulled away from our current activity. Even if we choose not to engage with the notification immediately, our mind is momentarily distracted, wondering about the content of the message or alert.

This pattern of constant interruption can lead to what's known as 'attention residue,' where our thoughts continue to linger on the previous task (or in this case, the notification) even as we attempt to refocus on our original activity. As a result, our productivity and overall well-being can suffer.

What Are Mindful Notifications?

In contrast to traditional notifications, mindful notifications are designed to help us engage with technology in a more conscious, controlled manner. They're about creating a digital environment where we dictate the terms of engagement rather than being at the mercy of every incoming alert.

Mindful notifications aren't necessarily about reducing the number of notifications (although that can certainly be a part of it). Instead, they're about changing the way we interact with these digital interruptions.

Implementing Mindful Notifications

Let's now explore some practical strategies to cultivate the practice of mindful notifications:

Audit Your Notifications: Start by taking inventory of all the different types of notifications you receive on a typical day. This includes everything from emails and social media updates to app alerts and news bulletins. Ask yourself: Which of these truly add value to my day? Which ones align with my priorities and which ones serve merely as distractions?

Customize Your Settings: Once you've audited your notifications, adjust your settings accordingly. Most devices and applications allow you to customize your notifications, so you choose what, when, and how you're alerted. You might decide to disable notifications for certain apps entirely or specify 'do not disturb' periods during your day.

Pause Before Responding: When you receive a notification, make it a habit to take a moment before responding. This pause gives you the opportunity to decide whether this notification warrants immediate attention or whether it can wait.

Mindful Check-Ins: Instead of constantly reacting to incoming alerts, schedule specific times during your day for digital check-ins. This could be a designated time to check emails, social media, or other updates. Having set times for digital engagement reduces the constant pull of notifications and allows you to be more present in your day.

Utilize Do Not Disturb Features: Use features such as 'Do Not Disturb' or 'Focus Mode' available on most devices. These tools allow you to silence all notifications for a specified period, providing uninterrupted time to focus on a task, engage in meaningful face-to-face interaction, or simply relax.

Notification Mindfulness in Practice

Implementing mindful notifications is about returning control of your attention back into your hands. It allows you to engage with your digital environment on your terms, reducing the stress and distraction caused by constant interruptions.

Remember, it's not about completely eliminating all notifications—that's neither practical nor desirable in our modern, interconnected world. Instead, it's about finding a balance, a way to stay connected without letting these digital interactions dictate your day.

So as you navigate your digital world, consider introducing the practice of mindful notifications into your routine.

Start small, perhaps by turning off one or two non-essential notifications, and gradually build from there. Over time, you'll likely notice a shift in your digital habits—less mindless scrolling, less immediate reaction to every ping, and more mindful, intentional interaction with your devices.

And most importantly, remember that the goal of mindful notifications is not just about productivity, but overall well-being. By reclaiming control over your digital environment, you're also reclaiming space for calm, focus, and presence in your day. You're creating an opportunity to engage more deeply with the world around you, rather than constantly being pulled into the digital realm.

As you continue your tech detox journey, remember that each small step is a part of a larger process. The path to mindful tech use isn't always linear, and there may be setbacks along the way, but with patience and persistence, you can cultivate a healthier, more balanced relationship with technology.

The next time your device pings, take a moment. Breathe. Choose how you want to respond. Remember, your digital devices are tools, meant to serve you—not the other way around. With mindful notifications, you can start making that principle a reality in your everyday life.

The Mindful Screen Time: A Balancing Act

Screen time, in our digital age, is practically unavoidable. Screens have become an integral part of our daily lives—tools for work, communication, entertainment, and even learning. However, as many of us have experienced, screen time can easily tip from being beneficial to problematic. We may find ourselves mindlessly scrolling through social media feeds, binge-watching videos, or checking emails at all hours, leading to digital fatigue, stress, and disconnection from our immediate environment.

In this section, we'll explore how to find a healthier balance with screen time through mindfulness, turning this potential source of stress into an opportunity for greater awareness and well-being.

Understanding the Impact of Screen Time

Before we dive into strategies for mindful screen time, let's take a moment to consider why it's a concern.

Excessive or unregulated screen time can have several adverse effects, including physical issues like eye strain, sleep disturbances, and sedentary behavior. It can also contribute to mental health concerns such as increased stress, anxiety, and feelings of isolation.

Furthermore, when our screen time is dominated by mindless or passive consumption—think endless social media scrolling or back-to-back episodes of a TV show—we may miss out on opportunities for more fulfilling, creative, or interactive activities.

The Concept of Mindful Screen Time

Mindful screen time is about bringing intention and awareness to our digital interactions. It's not simply about reducing screen time, but about improving the quality of the time we spend with screens.

This means consciously choosing what we engage with, staying present and focused during that engagement, and regularly checking in with ourselves to assess how our screen activities are affecting our physical and emotional well-being.

Implementing Mindful Screen Time

Implementing mindful screen time requires a multi-faceted approach, and here are some strategies you might find helpful:

Set Clear Intentions: Before you unlock your device, pause for a moment. What's your intention for this screen time? Are you seeking to communicate, to work, to learn, to relax, or are you reaching for your device out of habit or boredom?

Single-Tasking: Our devices often tempt us into multitasking, but this can lead to scattered attention and diminished productivity. Try to do one thing at a time. If you're watching a video, just watch. If you're writing an email, just write.

Mindful Check-Ins: Regularly check in with yourself during screen time. Are you still aligned with your original intention? How are you feeling physically and emotionally? Use these insights to adjust your screen time as needed.

Digital-free Zones: Designate certain times and spaces in your home as screen-free. This might be during meals, the first hour after waking, the last hour before bed, or any time and place you want to dedicate to undistracted presence.

Quality Over Quantity: Prioritize activities that are meaningful and fulfilling. This might mean choosing to video chat with a friend over aimless browsing, or using an educational app instead of playing a mindless game.

The Balancing Act

Remember, mindful screen time is not about perfection. It's about creating a healthier balance and cultivating more conscious digital habits.

Some days you may find it easier to limit your screen time and stay focused. Other days, you might lose track of time on social media or fall into a binge-watching spiral. That's okay. The goal isn't to eliminate these behaviors completely, but to become more aware of them, understand their triggers and effects, and gradually shift towards healthier habits.

The journey to mindful screen time is just that—a journey. It involves learning, experimenting, making mistakes, and learning some more.

The most crucial aspect of this journey is remaining kind and patient with yourself. Remember, we're dealing with deeply ingrained habits here, ones that have been reinforced by the very design of our digital devices and platforms, which are often created to capture and hold our attention for as long as possible. It's natural to encounter resistance and setbacks along the way. When you do, rather than berating yourself, use these moments as opportunities for learning and growth.

Consider each moment of mindless screen time as a reminder to bring yourself back to mindfulness, in the same way that we return our attention to the breath during meditation when we notice it has wandered. Each return is a moment of mindfulness in itself, a reinforcement of your intention to stay present and conscious in your digital interactions.

Furthermore, keep in mind that mindful screen time is not a one-size-fits-all solution. We all have different digital needs and habits. Therefore, the application of the strategies mentioned above will look different for everyone. Customize these suggestions to fit your personal situation and lifestyle, and don't be afraid to experiment and adjust as you go along.

In the end, the goal of mindful screen time is to facilitate a more balanced, intentional, and conscious relationship with our digital devices. A relationship where we use these tools for our benefit without letting them dominate our lives or our attention. By integrating the principles of mindfulness, we can navigate our digital world with more ease, awareness, and autonomy.

Mindful screen time, as a concept, extends to all areas of our digital interactions, serving as a foundational skill in our tech detox journey. So, whether you're checking your emails, posting on social media, or watching your favorite show, remember: be present, be intentional, and most importantly, be kind to yourself.

Chapter 6: The Emerging Field of Digital Minimalism

What is Digital Minimalism and Why it Matters?

As we delve into Chaour Tech Detox journey, let's start to unpack a concept that's been gaining momentum in recent years: digital minimalism. It's not only a buzzword that seems to get thrown around in modern discourse, but it's also an emerging field that's both challenging and reshaping our relationship with technology.

So, what exactly is digital minimalism? Well, simply put, digital minimalism is a philosophy that encourages the thoughtful and purposeful use of digital technologies. It urges us to engage with our devices and applications in a way that directly serves our values, needs, and life goals, rather than letting them dictate our time and attention.

But it's not just about decluttering our digital lives or reducing screen time. It's about intentionality, agency, and a deep sense of purpose. It's about asking ourselves the hard questions: What value does this technology provide me? Does it align with my life goals and personal values? Is it helping or hindering my wellbeing?

Digital minimalism is about redefining our relationship with technology, not severing it entirely. It recognizes that in the digital age, complete disconnection isn't just unrealistic; it's also potentially unbeneficial. After all, technology can be a wonderful tool. It can connect us, inform us, entertain us, and even aid us in personal development. The issue arises, however, when it starts to control us, to erode our ability to concentrate, to be present, and to engage with the world around us fully.

Why does digital minimalism matter? Why is it important enough to be addressed in this book? There are a multitude of reasons, but let's focus on the key ones.

Firstly, we live in an age of constant digital bombardment. Every day, we're exposed to an influx of information and stimulation, from social media notifications and emails, to news updates and digital ads. All of this is fighting for our attention, and it's exhausting. It can cause us to feel overwhelmed, anxious, and perpetually distracted. Digital minimalism offers a counterbalance to this, a way of managing our digital consumption without feeling like we're drowning in it.

Secondly, the way we use technology can deeply impact our physical and mental health. Excessive screen time can lead to eye strain, poor posture, and sleep disturbances, while the constant connectivity can exacerbate stress levels, lead to burnout, and even contribute to the development of mental health issues like depression and anxiety. Digital minimalism promotes healthier tech habits that prioritize our wellbeing.

Thirdly, embracing digital minimalism can free up time, allowing us to spend it on things that truly matter. Instead of mindlessly scrolling through social media or getting lost in the rabbit hole of online content, we can engage in activities that enrich our lives, be it reading, writing, spending time with loved ones, exercising, or simply being present in the moment.

Lastly, digital minimalism fosters a sense of autonomy. It empowers us to make mindful decisions about our digital consumption, rather than being at the mercy of algorithms and the latest tech trends. This sense of control can improve our self-esteem and overall life satisfaction.

However, it's important to note that digital minimalism isn't a one-size-fits-all solution. It's a flexible philosophy that can be adapted based on individual needs, goals, and circumstances. Some people might find value in significantly reducing their digital footprint, while others might find it more beneficial to curate their digital interactions carefully.

In the end, it's all about finding a balance - a way to coexist with technology that benefits us, enriches our lives, and align with our personal values and life goals.

Now that we understand what digital minimalism is and why it matters, it's worth taking a moment to consider its broader societal implications. We exist in an era where technology is rapidly advancing, where the next big app or gadget seems to emerge almost daily. In this whirlwind of innovation, it's easy to get swept up in the digital current. However, digital minimalism urges us to pause, to assess, and to make mindful choices. It presents an alternative to the mainstream narrative of 'more is better' when it comes to digital consumption.

This alternative isn't just important on an individual level; it's crucial on a societal scale too. As we begin to grapple with the consequences of unchecked digital consumption — ranging from the mental health crisis to issues of privacy and data security — adopting a more mindful, intentional approach towards technology can be a game-changer.

The idea behind digital minimalism is not to demonize technology, but rather to promote a healthier, more balanced relationship with it. This approach acknowledges the significant role that technology plays in our lives, while also recognizing the potential harm it can cause when its use is unchecked.

At its core, digital minimalism is about redefining success in the digital age. It argues that success isn't about having the latest gadgets, being constantly connected, or being 'online' 24/7. Instead, success is about using technology in a way that serves us — that enriches our lives, helps us achieve our goals, and aligns with our values. It's about quality, not quantity, depth, not breadth.

Remember, the aim is not to prescribe a rigid set of rules, but rather to provide a framework that can be adapted and modified to fit your unique circumstances and needs. The ultimate goal is to empower you to reclaim control over your digital life and to foster a healthier, more balanced, and more fulfilling relationship with technology.

I invite you to take a moment to reflect on your own digital habits. How do you currently interact with technology? Do you feel in control of your digital life, or does it control you? How would your life look different if you adopted a digital minimalism approach? Ponder on these questions, and carry them with you as we embark on the practical journey of digital minimalism. And remember, the road to digital minimalism isn't about reaching a destination — it's about the journey, the mindful choices you make each day, and the peace and balance that comes with them.

Techniques and Practices for Digital Minimalism

Embracing digital minimalism may seem like a daunting task, especially considering how integrated technology has become in our daily lives. However, with the right strategies and a bit of discipline, it's a thoroughly achievable goal. Let's explore some techniques and practices that can help guide you on your digital minimalism journey.

Digital Declutter: The first step towards digital minimalism is decluttering. Start by evaluating your digital habits and the technologies you use daily. Do they align with your life goals and values? Are they providing value, or merely acting as distractions? Start removing or reducing non-essential apps, notifications, and digital interactions. Declutter your email inbox, your social media feeds, and your smartphone. This not only reduces distractions but also helps clear your digital environment, making it easier to focus on what truly matters.

Intentional Tech Use: Aim to use technology with a specific purpose in mind, rather than mindlessly browsing or scrolling. If you're going to use social media, have a clear idea of what you want to achieve – be it connecting with a friend, getting updates on a particular topic, or sharing something meaningful. Intentionality is a crucial aspect of digital minimalism.

Scheduled Offline Time: Carving out specific times in your day for being offline can be incredibly beneficial. These digital-free zones could include mealtimes, the first hour after waking up, or the last hour before bed. You could also designate a full day each week (or month) as a tech-free day, where you disconnect entirely and indulge in non-digital activities.

Mindful Notifications: Notifications can be a significant source of digital stress, constantly pulling your attention away from whatever you're doing. Audit your notification settings – do you really need to be notified every time someone likes your post or sends an email? Customize your notifications to allow only the most important ones to interrupt you.

Mindful Social Media Use: Social media can be a valuable tool for staying connected, but it can also be a major time sink and source of stress. Consider reducing the number of platforms you use, unfollowing accounts that don't provide value or joy, and setting limits on how much time you spend on these platforms each day.

Tech-Free Zones: Designate certain areas in your home as tech-free zones. This could be your bedroom, a reading corner, or even the dining room table. Having physical spaces that are free from digital distractions can help cultivate a sense of calm and presence.

Prioritizing Non-Digital Activities: Engage more in non-digital activities that you enjoy, like reading physical books, writing in a journal, hiking, or playing a musical instrument. These activities can provide a healthy balance to your digital life and can be deeply fulfilling.

Digital Detox Periods: Every now and then, consider taking a complete break from digital devices. This could be for a weekend, a week, or even a month. A digital detox can help reset your digital habits and provide a refreshing perspective on your relationship with technology.

Mindful Consumption of Online Content: Be mindful of the content you consume online. Is it adding value to your life? Is it inspiring, educational, or uplifting? Or is it simply filling time? Aim to consume content that aligns with your values and contributes positively to your life.

Digital Minimalism Tools and Apps: Ironically, there are digital tools designed to help with digital minimalism. These include website blockers, time tracking apps, and social media usage monitors. Use these tools as aids on your journey towards mindful tech use.

Single-Tasking: In the digital age, we've become masters of multitasking, often at the expense of our productivity and mental well-being. Try to focus on one task at a time, whether it's reading an article, writing an email, or engaging in a conversation. This will not only improve your productivity but also help reduce digital fatigue and stress.

Mindfulness and Meditation: Mindfulness and meditation can help you cultivate a greater sense of presence and awareness, which can be incredibly beneficial when trying to reduce digital distractions. Even a few minutes of mindfulness or meditation each day can make a significant difference.

Embracing Boredom: In our always-connected world, we've come to dread boredom. However, boredom can be a powerful catalyst for creativity and self-reflection. Instead of reaching for your phone the moment you have nothing to do, try sitting with your boredom and see where it leads you.

Setting Clear Boundaries: Set clear boundaries for when and how you use technology. This could include no screens during family meals, turning off work email notifications after a certain time, or keeping your phone out of your bedroom. Boundaries can help ensure technology doesn't encroach on every aspect of your life.

Regular Reflection and Adjustment: Regularly reflect on your digital habits and adjust as needed. Digital minimalism is not a static state but a continual process of evaluation and adjustment. As your life circumstances change, your digital needs and habits may also need to change.

These are just a few techniques and practices for embracing digital minimalism. The key is to find what works best for you. What practices resonate most with your lifestyle, values, and goals? Remember, digital minimalism isn't about following a strict set of rules; it's about crafting a digital life that aligns with who you are and how you want to live.

It isn't about perfection or completely eliminating technology from our lives. It's about fostering a more balanced, healthier relationship with technology. It's about regaining control over our digital lives, focusing on what truly adds value, and letting go of the digital clutter that doesn't.

The goal of digital minimalism isn't to restrict or limit joy but to create space for more meaningful, fulfilling experiences – both online and offline. It's about choosing to interact with technology on your terms, with intentionality and purpose. It's about choosing quality over quantity, depth over breadth, and purpose over mindless consumption.

As you embark on your digital minimalism journey, remember to be patient with yourself. It's a process, and like any significant life change, it requires time, effort, and patience. But with every small step you take, you'll be closer to living a more mindful, intentional, and balanced digital life.

Case Studies: Successful Digital Minimalists

Examining real-world examples of individuals who have successfully adopted digital minimalism can offer not just inspiration, but also practical insights into how this philosophy can be implemented. Let's delve into some case studies of successful digital minimalists.
(Full names have been withheld to protect the privacy of the individuals)

Case Study 1: The Mindful Entrepreneur

Meet Sara, an entrepreneur running her own digital marketing company. Her job demands she be continuously updated with the latest trends and constantly connected to her team and clients. However, she began to feel overwhelmed with the amount of time she spent online and started experiencing burnout.

Sara took the bold step to explore digital minimalism. She began by auditing her digital consumption, pinpointing the platforms and activities that were consuming most of her time but not adding significant value. She unsubscribed from unnecessary newsletters, reduced the frequency of her social media checks, and turned off non-essential notifications. She introduced tech-free zones at home, especially during mealtimes and the hour before bedtime. Moreover, she decided to dedicate the first two hours of her day to strategic thinking and planning without using any digital devices.

Her changes didn't go unnoticed. Sara began to feel less overwhelmed, her sleep improved, and she found she had more time for her personal hobbies and family. She reported increased productivity at work as she could focus better on her tasks without constant distractions. By adopting digital minimalism, Sara could maintain her digital presence without letting it control her life.

Case Study 2: The Student in Balance

Next, let's consider Tom, a university student. With lectures, research, assignments, and a social life primarily revolving around digital platforms, he felt perpetually glued to screens. He noticed he was struggling with concentration, suffering from regular headaches, and losing touch with non-digital hobbies he used to enjoy.

Intrigued by the idea of digital minimalism, Tom decided to experiment. He started by designating specific hours for studying without any digital distractions. He made a rule to close all unrelated tabs while studying online and used an app to block distracting websites during his study hours. Tom also chose to leave his phone behind when going for a meal or a walk, using this as a break from constant digital connectivity.

The effects were remarkable. Tom found his concentration improving, his stress levels reducing, and he even started enjoying his old hobbies like reading physical books and playing guitar. Digital minimalism allowed Tom to utilize technology effectively for his studies while enjoying a balanced life.

Case Study 3: The Conscious Creative

Now let's look at Maya, a freelance graphic designer. Social media platforms were a significant part of her work life, not just for inspiration but also for networking and showcasing her work. However, Maya realized that her screen time was skyrocketing, and her creativity was suffering due to digital overload.

Embracing digital minimalism, Maya started to limit her social media usage to certain times in the day and decided to keep weekends entirely social-media-free. She chose to mute notifications from social media apps and check them at her convenience. Maya also started dedicating more time to non-digital forms of creativity, like sketching and painting.

As a result, Maya noticed that her creative energy surged. She was less anxious, more focused, and found joy in her work again. By strategically using social media and dedicating time for offline creativity, Maya found her balance through digital minimalism.

Case Study 4: The Tech-Savvy Parent

Consider the example of David, a father of two teenagers, struggling to manage his kids' screen time and his own. Being a software engineer, technology was a huge part of his life. Yet, he felt disconnected from his family due to the constant presence of screens during their family time. He also found himself mindlessly browsing through his phone during his downtime.

David decided to implement digital minimalism principles within his family. They began with no-device dinners, ensuring that their meal times were focused on face-to-face conversation. He also initiated tech-free weekends where the family would engage in outdoor activities, board games, and other non-digital pursuits. For himself, David chose to set defined boundaries for work and created designated times to check his emails and messages, reducing constant distractions.

As a result, David noticed a significant increase in quality time spent with his family. His children, too, seemed to enjoy the tech-free activities and became more conscious of their screen time. David found that he could focus better on his work without the constant need to check his phone.

Case Study 5: The Active Retiree

Let's also look at a different demographic through Patricia, a retired teacher. Patricia found herself spending a lot of time watching TV, surfing the internet, and playing online games. While these activities helped her feel connected and occupied initially, over time she felt it was taking a toll on her mental and physical health.

Intrigued by digital minimalism, Patricia decided to bring some changes into her life. She chose to limit her TV time to specific shows she genuinely enjoyed and reduced her random internet surfing, replacing it with dedicated time for reading and gardening. She also started using her phone more for audio and video calls to her friends and family, rather than just text messages or social media interactions.

The impact was profound. Patricia felt more active and engaged in her daily life. She started enjoying her reading sessions and her time in the garden. Her friends and family also appreciated the personal calls, which made Patricia feel more connected and less isolated.

Case Study 6: The High-Flying Executive

Now, let's turn our attention to Rebecca, a top-level executive in a multinational corporation. She had become accustomed to an incessant flow of work emails, conference calls, and instant messages, maintaining a near-constant digital presence. However, Rebecca started experiencing heightened stress levels, insomnia, and a sense of disconnection from her personal life.

Intrigued by the concept of digital minimalism, she decided to make some changes. She set strict boundaries for her work communications, dedicating specific hours for checking emails and responding to messages. She turned off work notifications after work hours and during the weekends. Additionally, she made a conscious effort to take regular tech breaks throughout her day, using this time to take a walk, meditate, or simply rest.

The results were highly beneficial. Rebecca noticed a significant reduction in her stress levels, an improvement in her sleep quality, and more time and energy for her personal life. Despite her high-demand job, she found that digital minimalism provided her with a much-needed balance.

Case Study 7: The Independent Artist

Our last example is of Leo, an independent musician and composer. Social media was an integral part of Leo's work, allowing him to share his creations, network with fellow musicians, and connect with his fanbase. However, he felt overwhelmed with the pressure to constantly post updates and engage with his followers.

Leo decided to adopt digital minimalism in an attempt to regain control over his digital life. He chose specific times of the day for social media engagement and limited his use of these platforms outside these slots. He also opted to turn off notifications from social media apps and started dedicating more time to offline music creation.

This shift towards digital minimalism was transformative for Leo. He felt more in control of his online presence, less pressured to continually engage, and more importantly, he found himself spending more quality time on his music.

These case studies illustrate the transformative potential of digital minimalism. They show that regardless of your profession, lifestyle, or age, embracing digital minimalism can lead to a more balanced, focused, and fulfilling life. Whether you're an entrepreneur, a student, a designer, a parent, a retiree, an executive, or an artist, digital minimalism offers a way to reclaim your time, focus, and energy from the pervasive pull of digital distractions. It provides an approach to engaging with digital technologies that is conscious, intentional, and grounded in respect for personal well-being and life values.

Through the stories of these successful digital minimalists, we can see that digital minimalism isn't a rigid ideology but a flexible, adaptable philosophy that can be tailored to suit individual needs, circumstances, and aspirations. It's not about rejecting technology outright but about establishing a healthier, more mindful relationship with it - a relationship where we control our technology, not the other way around. It's about using them consciously, intentionally, in ways that serve us and align with our individual needs, goals, and lifestyle.

It's a personalized, flexible approach that promotes well-being, balance, and intentional living in the digital age. And as we see, the benefits of this mindful approach can be significant and transformative.

Minimalism and Mindfulness: A Perfect Pair

Minimalism and mindfulness may appear to be two separate concepts, yet they intersect beautifully, particularly in the realm of our digital lives. As we've delved into digital minimalism and its practices, you might have noticed how closely it aligns with the principles of mindfulness. Both these philosophies ultimately aim to enhance the quality of our lives, bringing about more focus, balance, and intentionality.

Let's break down how these two concepts intertwine and together, how they can create a more enriching digital life experience.

Shared Values:

At their core, both minimalism and mindfulness emphasize living intentionally. They encourage us to slow down and make conscious decisions about what we allow into our lives. Where minimalism asks us to declutter our lives of non-essential possessions (or in the case of digital minimalism, digital engagements), mindfulness asks us to be fully present in our actions, thoughts, and feelings. Both suggest we focus on what truly matters, cutting out the unnecessary noise and clutter.

Complementary Practices:

Minimalism and mindfulness aren't just shared in philosophy; their practices can also support and enhance each other. For instance, the mindfulness practice of meditation can be incredibly beneficial for those aiming to adopt digital minimalism. By training your mind to focus and resist distractions, meditation can make it easier to ignore the digital "buzz" and stay focused on meaningful tasks.

On the other hand, the decluttering practices of minimalism can enhance mindfulness by creating a more peaceful, distraction-free environment conducive to mindful living. As we minimize digital distractions, it becomes easier to engage in mindful practices like deep, focused work or mindful eating.

Mindful Consumption:

Another area where minimalism and mindfulness intersect is mindful consumption. In the digital context, this means being discerning about the digital content we consume. Just as mindfulness encourages us to eat mindfully, savoring each bite, digital minimalism encourages us to consume digital content mindfully, selecting only what truly adds value to our lives and savoring it without rushing or multitasking.

Shared Benefits:

Both minimalism and mindfulness offer similar benefits - increased focus, reduced stress, more time and energy for what truly matters. By adopting digital minimalism, we can enjoy these benefits in our digital lives. We can move away from mindless scrolling, constant distractions, and digital overload, and towards a digital life that's more focused, balanced, and fulfilling.

A Unified Approach:

Taken together, minimalism and mindfulness offer a unified approach to living well in the digital age. They provide us with a roadmap to navigate the digital world in a way that respects our well-being, values, and personal goals. They show us how we can use digital technologies not mindlessly or excessively, but mindfully and minimally, extracting their benefits without getting overwhelmed by their potential downsides.

In the age of digital excess, the combined practices of digital minimalism and mindfulness can serve as a beacon, guiding us towards a more balanced, intentional, and fulfilling digital life. They can help us navigate the digital landscape with discernment and intention, ensuring our digital experiences align with our life goals and values.

In this way, minimalism and mindfulness indeed form a perfect pair, offering a holistic approach to mindful living in the digital age.

Chapter 7: Staying Committed: Strategies for a Sustainable Tech Detox

Addressing Roadblocks: The Role of Mindful Resilience

Just as the best of journeys has its bumps and detours, your tech detox adventure is bound to meet with obstacles. These challenges, however, do not spell disaster. Instead, they present an opportunity to develop mindful resilience, an essential quality that will ensure your continued commitment to a balanced digital lifestyle.

First, let's examine what we mean by "mindful resilience". Resilience, at its core, is the ability to bounce back from adversity. It's about weathering the storm, and coming out on the other side, maybe a bit battered, but still standing. Mindful resilience takes this concept a step further, marrying it with mindfulness, or the conscious act of focusing our attention on the present moment without judgment.

So, what does mindful resilience look like in the context of a tech detox? It means not berating yourself when you find your fingers involuntarily reaching for your smartphone. It means recognising that your impulse to check your email during dinner is just that – an impulse, not a command. It means maintaining your resolve in the face of setbacks, learning from each experience, and continuously adjusting your strategies for better outcomes.

Let's explore some common roadblocks you may encounter during your tech detox journey and practical strategies for overcoming them.

Roadblock 1: FOMO – Fear of Missing Out

FOMO, or Fear of Missing Out, is a significant barrier that many people face when reducing their digital dependency. This fear can be pervasive, creeping into your thoughts and influencing your behavior. "What if there's an important email?" "What if I miss out on a fun event my friends are attending?" "What if there's breaking news?"

The first step to combating FOMO is to recognise it for what it is: a fear, not a reality. Most of the time, what we fear missing out on isn't as essential or rewarding as we perceive it to be. We can address this by setting aside specific times to check our devices, perhaps once in the morning and once in the evening. By structuring our engagement with technology, we can alleviate some of the anxiety associated with FOMO.

Mindfulness techniques can also be beneficial. When you notice feelings of FOMO creeping in, instead of succumbing to them, try to pause and observe your feelings without judgment. Ask yourself, "Is this fear rational? Will I truly miss out on something important if I don't check my phone right now?"

Roadblock 2: Dependence on Tech for Stress Relief

Technology can be an attractive escape from daily stressors. Whether it's mindlessly scrolling through social media feeds or immersing ourselves in the latest mobile game, these digital distractions offer a temporary reprieve from our worries.

However, this type of stress relief is usually short-lived and can often exacerbate feelings of stress in the long run. Instead, consider swapping out some of these digital coping mechanisms for more mindful activities. Things like going for a walk, practicing yoga, or even just sitting quietly with your thoughts can offer a far more meaningful and lasting form of relaxation.

Roadblock 3: Societal Expectations

Living in a digital age, societal expectations can also pose a significant roadblock to your tech detox journey. The instant-response culture, the 24/7 work availability, and the constant need to stay "connected" can make it difficult to detach from our devices.

One way to address this challenge is by setting boundaries and clearly communicating them with your colleagues, friends, and family. Let them know about your tech detox goals and the specific times you've dedicated to digital disconnection. It's also essential to remember that setting these boundaries isn't just about informing others; it's about sticking to them yourself. So when you're on your tech-free time, truly be in that moment, unencumbered by digital distractions.

Roadblock 4: Lack of Accountability

When we embark on a journey alone, it's easier to let ourselves off the hook. This lack of accountability can cause us to slide back into old habits. A solution here could be to find a tech-detox buddy. It could be a friend, a family member, or even a co-worker who also wants to find a more balanced relationship with technology. When you have someone to share your struggles and triumphs with, you'll find it easier to stay committed to your goals.

Roadblock 5: Unrealistic Expectations

This final roadblock is possibly the most insidious because it comes from within. You might start your detox journey with the best of intentions, only to find yourself dismayed when you don't instantly become a Zen master of mindful living. Remember, it's not about achieving perfection; it's about progress.

Setting smaller, more achievable goals can be helpful here. Rather than aiming to completely eliminate screen time, try to reduce it gradually. Perhaps start with an hour of device-free time each day, then build up from there. Recognize and celebrate each victory, no matter how small, and forgive yourself for the slip-ups.

Ultimately, your tech detox journey is about creating a healthier, more mindful relationship with technology. And it's this mindfulness that will guide you through the roadblocks, making you more resilient each step of the way.

In our digital age, complete and total disconnection is neither practical nor desirable. The aim isn't to demonize technology but to ensure we're using it in a way that supports our wellbeing, rather than detracting from it. When we bring mindfulness to our digital interactions, we can start to use technology as a tool that serves us, rather than feeling like we're at its mercy.

Your tech detox journey may not always be smooth sailing, but it's a journey worth taking. And with the strategies discussed in this chapter, you'll be well-equipped to tackle any obstacles that come your way. So, here's to mindful resilience – your trusty compass guiding you towards a healthier digital life.

Creating a Mindful Digital Environment: Home and Work

A mindful digital environment is one where technology serves you, not the other way around. It's a space where devices are tools, not masters, where interactions with technology are purposeful, not mindless. Creating such an environment, both at home and at work, is a crucial step in maintaining your tech detox journey. Here are a few strategies to help you get there.

At Home: A Sanctuary of Mindfulness

Home is where we recharge our batteries, both literally and figuratively. It should be a space of relaxation and respite, where we can escape from the demands of the outside world. However, it's often here that we mindlessly reach for our devices, scrolling through social media, catching up on news, or binge-watching our favorite series. How then, can we transform our homes into sanctuaries of mindfulness?

1. Designated Device-Free Zones

Consider creating areas in your home that are designated device-free zones. These could be spaces dedicated to relaxation, such as your bedroom or a cozy reading nook. By keeping these areas free of digital distractions, you allow yourself space to engage in mindful activities, such as reading, writing, meditating, or simply enjoying a cup of tea.

2. Scheduled Tech Breaks

Establish regular tech breaks, where all devices are put away, and attention is focused on non-digital activities. These could be during meal times or a few hours before bed. It not only gives your mind a break from the constant stream of digital information but also encourages more meaningful interaction with family members.

3. Mindful Usage of Devices

When you do use your devices at home, strive to do so mindfully. Rather than mindlessly scrolling, try to use your devices for a specific purpose. It could be to learn something new, connect with a friend, or plan your next vacation.

At Work: Balancing Productivity and Well-being

The workplace is where we are often most tethered to our devices. Emails, reports, video conferences, instant messaging – our work lives are deeply intertwined with technology. However, even in this environment, we can create pockets of mindfulness.

Staying Committed: Strategies for a Sustainable Tech Detox

1. Mindful Communication

A large portion of our digital interactions at work involves communication – emails, instant messages, video calls. Instead of constantly checking for new messages or responding immediately to every email, try scheduling specific times during your day for these tasks. This approach can help minimize distractions and allow you to concentrate more effectively on your work.

2. Digital Breaks

Just as at home, it's important to take regular digital breaks at work too. Use this time to stand up, stretch, or even take a short walk outside. These moments can act as mini-refreshers, helping you maintain your focus and productivity throughout the day.

3. Mindful Meetings

In the era of back-to-back video meetings, it's important to maintain mindfulness even during these digital interactions. One way to achieve this is by ensuring you have at least 10-15 minutes between meetings. Use this time to mentally prepare for the next meeting, or simply relax and recharge.

4. Setting Boundaries

Just as you did with your personal life, communicate your tech boundaries at work too. It's okay to let your colleagues know that you won't be checking emails after a certain time or over the weekends. Remember, you're entitled to a work-life balance.

Digital Aesthetics

This is a lesser-discussed aspect of our digital environment, but one that can make a significant difference. The aesthetics of our digital tools can affect our mood and mindset. Choose calming wallpapers for your desktop or smartphone. Organize your files and folders in a way that makes your workspace feel uncluttered and inviting. Even something as simple as choosing a pleasing font for your documents can subtly enhance your digital experience.

Mindful Consumption

In our digital world, we're not just consumers of technology; we're also consumers of digital content. News, social media, videos, podcasts – there's a constant influx of information, and it's all too easy to consume mindlessly. Practice mindful consumption by choosing quality content that enriches your life. Be discerning, and don't be afraid to unsubscribe or unfollow sources that don't add value to your life.

Digital Tools for Mindfulness

There are numerous apps and programs designed to promote mindfulness and well-being. From meditation apps like Headspace and Calm to digital minimalism tools that help reduce online distractions, these can be powerful allies on your tech detox journey.

In creating a mindful digital environment, both at home and at work, remember the key principle: Intentionality. Every choice you make, every boundary you set, every practice you adopt should be done with a clear purpose. By doing so, you shift from being a passive consumer of technology to an active and mindful participant in the digital age.

It's an ongoing process, and there will be times when you falter, and that's okay. The goal isn't perfection but progress. With each mindful choice, you're forging a healthier relationship with technology, one that honors both your need for connectivity and your inherent need for peace and well-being

Creating a mindful digital environment both at home and at work is about making conscious choices. It's about integrating technology into your life in a way that supports your well-being, not at the expense of it. It may take some effort to establish these practices, but once you do, you'll find that you're not just surviving in the digital era, you're thriving.

The Digital Diet: Strategies for Healthier Tech Consumption

Just as we maintain a balanced diet to nourish our bodies, a balanced digital diet is key to nurturing our minds. Understanding and moderating our tech consumption is critical for our mental and emotional health. In this section, we'll delve into what a healthy digital diet looks like and provide strategies to help you achieve it.

Understanding the Digital Diet

The concept of a digital diet isn't about severe restriction or digital starvation; rather, it's about intentional and mindful consumption. This concept applies to the type, quality, and quantity of digital content we consume daily. When we talk about a balanced digital diet, we're looking at both reducing digital junk food—those mindless scrolling activities that add little value—and adding more digital superfoods—purposeful and enriching digital interactions.

Digital Junk Food vs. Digital Superfoods

Just like food, not all digital content is created equal. It's essential to discern between digital junk food and digital superfoods.

Staying Committed: Strategies for a Sustainable Tech Detox

Digital junk food refers to content that offers little nutritional value for our minds. Think of mindless scrolling on social media, sensational news stories, click-bait articles, or binge-watching episodes of a show late into the night. These activities can leave us feeling drained, anxious, or unsatisfied, much like the aftermath of indulging in too much junk food.

On the other hand, digital superfoods are those digital activities that nourish our minds and spirits. They are the digital equivalent of a hearty salad or a refreshing smoothie. This could be learning a new skill through an online course, watching an inspiring TED talk, listening to an educational podcast, or using a meditation app. These activities add value to our lives and leave us feeling enriched and satisfied.

Strategies for a Balanced Digital Diet

Intentional Consumption: Start by being more mindful about why you're reaching for your device. Is it out of boredom? Procrastination? Habit? By identifying the triggers, you can begin to break the cycle of mindless use.

Scheduled Screen Time: Allocate specific times of the day for using technology. This structured approach can help you stay focused on your digital activities and resist the urge to mindlessly check your devices.

Quality Over Quantity: Prioritize digital activities that bring you joy, teach you something new, or help you stay connected with loved ones. Cut down on activities that lead to anxiety, comparison, or dissatisfaction.

Digital Detox: Regularly schedule digital detox days or weekends. Use this time to engage in non-digital activities you love or explore new hobbies. This break gives your mind a much-needed rest and helps reset your digital habits.

Use Tools to Help: Make use of apps and settings designed to promote healthier tech habits. Screen-time trackers can give you insight into how much time you're spending on different activities, while app limit settings can help you manage your usage.

Remember, a balanced digital diet is not about completely eliminating certain digital activities—it's about creating a healthier relationship with technology.

So go ahead, indulge in that funny cat video or social media catch-up, but balance it with digital superfoods that truly nourish you. Your digital diet is in your hands. Choose wisely, consume mindfully, and don't forget to enjoy your digital meal.

Breaking Free: New Research on Long-term Benefits of Tech Detox

As we strive for balance and mindfulness in our digital consumption, it's valuable to understand the science behind the benefits of a tech detox. In this section, we delve into new research showing the long-term benefits of reducing our dependency on digital devices.

Improved Mental Health

Recent studies have shown a clear correlation between heavy technology use and mental health issues such as anxiety, depression, and stress. One study found that participants who cut back on social media use showed significant reductions in feelings of loneliness and depression. When we limit our exposure to negative digital environments and focus more on real-life interactions, we tend to experience improved mental health.

Better Sleep Quality

Research also highlights the impact of technology on sleep. The blue light emitted by screens suppresses the secretion of melatonin, a hormone that regulates sleep. A tech detox, particularly before bedtime, can significantly improve sleep quality, leading to increased alertness and better overall health.

Enhanced Productivity

Our brains are not wired for the kind of multitasking that constant device use requires. Switching back and forth between tasks can reduce productivity by as much as 40%. By reducing unnecessary digital interruptions, we allow our brains to focus more deeply on tasks, leading to improved productivity and creativity.

Improved Physical Health

Decreased screen time can also lead to improved physical health. Excessive device use has been linked to a sedentary lifestyle, contributing to obesity and associated health risks. By breaking free from our screens, we naturally become more active, leading to better physical health.

Increased Real-Life Interactions

Human beings are social creatures, and meaningful face-to-face interactions are essential for our well-being. By cutting back on virtual communications and focusing more on real-life interactions, we can improve our relationships and our overall life satisfaction.

Developing Mindful Habits

The act of engaging in a tech detox also has the potential to cultivate mindfulness. As we become more intentional in our technology use, we can extend that mindfulness to other aspects of our lives.

Staying Committed: Strategies for a Sustainable Tech Detox

Just as we learn to enjoy food without overindulging, we can learn to appreciate and utilize technology without being consumed by it.

As research continues to uncover the benefits of a tech detox, it becomes clear that our digital well-being is an essential component of our overall well-being. Breaking free from the constant onslaught of digital information allows our brains to reset, leading to improved mental, physical, and social health.

Chapter 8: The Future of Mindful Living in the Digital Age

The Rise of Tech-free Zones and Their Impact

We live in an era marked by a dichotomy of sorts. On the one hand, technology is penetrating all areas of our lives, bringing with it a deluge of conveniences. On the other hand, a growing section of society is striving to strike a balance, recognizing the need for moments of disconnection, leading to the creation of 'tech-free zones'. These spaces, essentially a no-device-land, represent a tectonic shift in our approach to living with technology.

With this chapter, let's delve into the future, exploring how these tech-free zones are sprouting up in various corners of our lives, and more importantly, understanding the impact they can have on our overall wellbeing.

The Emergence of Tech-Free Zones

Ironically, the concept of tech-free zones arises from the very heart of our technological utopia. Tech-free zones are spaces - physical or virtual - specifically designed to be free of digital devices, internet connectivity, and the cacophony of digital alerts. They can be as small as a corner in your home designated for reading, meditation, or simply quiet contemplation, or as large as tech-free retreats and holidays, where participants willingly disconnect from the digital world.

In an era where smartphones are appendages to our bodies, and smart devices permeate our homes and workplaces, these tech-free zones are radical. They challenge the hyper-connected norm, carving out sanctuaries of quiet amidst the relentless barrage of information.

Why is this trend emerging? Well, the answer is quite straightforward. The omnipresence of technology in our lives has led to an unprecedented level of digital fatigue, forcing us to reevaluate our relationship with it. This fatigue, stemming from prolonged screen time, the bombardment of notifications, and the 'always-on' expectation, has sparked a desire to disconnect, even if just for a brief period each day.

The Impact of Tech-Free Zones

The emergence of tech-free zones signifies a considerable shift in our collective mindset. It shows our recognition of the side-effects of technology overuse and our willingness to take steps to alleviate them. The impact of these zones, however, extends far beyond just acknowledging the need for a tech detox.

Mental Well-being

Unplugging from technology, even briefly, can do wonders for our mental health. It's a much-needed respite for our brains from the sensory overload that the digital world often imposes. A study published in the Journal of Environmental Psychology found that spending time in tech-free zones significantly reduces anxiety levels and improves overall mood. Moreover, these zones encourage mindfulness, allowing us to live in the moment rather than being consumed by digital distractions.

Physical Health

The health benefits of these zones are not confined to the mind; our bodies too bear the brunt of excessive technology use. Prolonged screen time can lead to a myriad of physical issues, such as eye strain, headaches, and postural problems. Regular disconnection can help alleviate these problems and promote healthier habits.

Productivity and Creativity

Surprisingly, stepping away from technology can actually boost our productivity and creativity. Studies suggest that constant interruptions from digital notifications hinder our ability to concentrate and think critically. By providing an oasis of quiet, tech-free zones allow our minds to focus, enhancing our cognitive abilities and fostering creativity.

Social Relationships

Let's not forget the social implications. Tech-free zones encourage face-to-face interaction and genuine connection, something that's often lost in our screen-dominated exchanges. They foster a sense of community, enhancing our social skills and empathy, and enabling deeper, more meaningful relationships.

The Future of Mindful Living in the Digital Age

As the awareness and acceptance of the potential side-effects of excessive technology use grow, we can anticipate the concept of tech-free zones to become more pervasive.

We might see more of these zones in our workplaces, fostering collaborative and creative thinking by removing digital interruptions. Schools could start implementing tech-free hours, encouraging children to engage in physical activities, creative play, and face-to-face interaction, fostering healthy habits from a young age. Citics might create tech-free parks - spaces where people can disconnect and engage with nature.

Additionally, we can expect an increase in tech-free retreats and vacations, as people recognize the value of truly 'switching off' and rejuvenating without the constant intrusion of technology.

Moreover, we might see a rise in tech products designed to promote tech-free living. Does that sound counterintuitive? Consider this - apps that limit screen time, or devices that block Wi-Fi signals in certain areas of the house during specified hours. As strange as it may sound, technology could well become the catalyst that enables us to detach from it.

The evolution of these tech-free zones may also give rise to new social norms. We might see 'digital etiquette' becoming commonplace - rules about when and where it's appropriate to use devices. A future where it's not unusual to see a sign saying "No Phones Allowed" at a cafe or a public park might not be far off.

The rise of tech-free zones is part of the broader movement towards mindful living in the digital age - a lifestyle that seeks to balance the benefits of technology with the need for mental peace and personal connection. This approach is not about completely shunning technology, but using it in a manner that enriches rather than dominates our lives.

In the grand scheme of things, tech-free zones could be seen as an antidote to our digital overdose. They offer a unique solution to our screen-addicted society, providing us with the chance to reset, rethink, and reconnect with the world around us.

Just as technology has become an integral part of our lives, the rise of tech-free zones heralds the beginning of a trend where deliberate disconnection becomes equally valued.

This movement isn't a regression or a resistance against technological progress, but rather a necessary counterbalance - an affirmation that while we embrace the digital, we also honor and protect our essential human nature.

And thus, the rise of tech-free zones could well be a defining aspect of mindful living in the digital age - an age where we appreciate technology for the wonders it can offer, while also recognizing the beauty of a moment of disconnection, a breath of tech-free air.

The Role of Tech Companies in Encouraging Mindful Use

With the understanding of the impact of tech-free zones and the benefits of mindful living in our grasp, it's worth asking - what role do tech companies, the architects of the digital world, play in this? Can they, or should they, actively encourage a more mindful use of their products?

The Awakening in Silicon Valley

Interestingly, there has been a remarkable shift in the tech industry's viewpoint. Some of the biggest players in the market have acknowledged the issue of tech overload and are beginning to implement features in their products that promote mindful use. This is not just a response to consumer demand, but an understanding of the ethical implications of their products and a desire to promote digital wellness.

For instance, giants like Google and Apple have incorporated "Digital Wellbeing" and "Screen Time" features into their operating systems, allowing users to monitor their device usage and set limits for individual apps. By offering insights into our digital behavior, these tools can serve as wake-up calls, encouraging us to be more mindful of how much time we're devoting to our screens.

Social media platforms, often considered the biggest culprits of tech addiction, have also started to take steps in this direction. Instagram, for example, introduced an activity dashboard that shows users the average time they spend on the app and allows them to set a daily usage limit.

Tech-Enabled Mindfulness

While it may seem counterintuitive, technology itself can actually be a powerful tool to encourage mindfulness. A growing number of apps, such as Headspace and Calm, are designed to promote mindfulness and mental well-being. These tools offer guided meditation, stress management techniques, sleep aids, and more. These initiatives reveal a promising trend where tech companies are investing in solutions that help users achieve a balance in their digital lives.

Shaping the Future of Tech Mindfulness

However, this is just the tip of the iceberg. There's much more that tech companies can - and should - do to foster mindful use. For one, they can continue to improve the visibility and effectiveness of digital wellness features. Making these tools more user-friendly and comprehensive can help users better understand their tech habits and take informed actions to modify them.

Furthermore, tech companies could also consider integrating 'tech-free' reminders or features into their devices - an alert that encourages users to take a break after a certain period of continuous usage, or a 'focus mode' that limits notifications for a specified time. These types of features can further encourage users to take regular tech breaks and engage in activities that don't involve screens.

It's also crucial for tech companies to practice transparency, particularly when it comes to algorithms that promote addictive behaviors, such as infinite scrolling or personalized recommendations. Educating users about these features and providing options to customize or disable them could go a long way in promoting mindful use.

Beyond the Screen

Finally, the role of tech companies shouldn't be limited to the virtual world. They can extend their influence to the physical world by promoting and supporting tech-free zones and activities. This could involve sponsoring tech-free events or retreats, advocating for digital wellness in schools and workplaces, or partnering with organizations that promote tech-life balance.

Tech companies play a crucial role in shaping our digital behaviors. Their commitment to encouraging mindful use is not just beneficial but necessary. While we as consumers need to take personal responsibility for our tech usage, the tools and environment that tech companies provide can significantly influence our ability to do so.

The rise of tech-free zones and the growing awareness of digital wellness represent a golden opportunity for these companies to redefine their role and contribute positively to the future of mindful living in the digital age.

Implications for Future Generations: Digital Citizenship

Our digital footprints have wider implications than we often realize, and as we navigate this constantly evolving digital landscape, we must also guide our younger generations towards becoming responsible digital citizens. This is a significant task that parents, educators, policymakers, and indeed, tech companies must undertake together.

Defining Digital Citizenship

Before we delve into the implications, it's crucial to define what we mean by 'Digital Citizenship.' In essence, digital citizenship refers to the responsible and respectful use of technology. It's about understanding the digital world, behaving appropriately in it, and knowing how to use technology in a way that's safe, ethical, and mindful. This concept encompasses a wide range of aspects, including digital literacy, online safety, cyber ethics, and importantly, digital wellness.

The Importance of Digital Citizenship

As technology continues to permeate our lives, it becomes increasingly important for future generations to understand their roles and responsibilities in the digital realm. Being a good digital citizen means more than just knowing how to use technology; it involves understanding the implications of our digital behaviors and making mindful decisions about our tech use.

Digital citizenship can equip future generations with the tools they need to navigate the digital world confidently and responsibly. It can teach them to balance the advantages of technology with the need for personal well-being and social interaction. It can empower them to use technology in a positive and productive way, rather than being passive consumers or, worse, victims of it.

The Role of Tech-Free Zones and Mindful Living

Tech-free zones and the principles of mindful living play a crucial role in fostering digital citizenship. These concepts can serve as practical tools for teaching future generations about digital balance and wellness.

For instance, having tech-free times at home or school can help children understand that while technology has its place, it's also important to have time away from screens. This can encourage them to engage in offline activities, foster their creativity, and improve their interpersonal skills.

Similarly, tech-free zones can also be a platform for discussing digital wellness and responsible tech use. By having open conversations about why these zones are necessary, we can raise awareness about the potential side-effects of excessive technology use and promote healthier digital habits.

The Future of Digital Citizenship

Looking ahead, digital citizenship is likely to become an integral part of our education system. We might see digital wellness and tech-life balance being included in school curriculums, with children being taught not only how to use technology, but also how to use it responsibly and mindfully.

Moreover, we can expect to see more collaboration between educators, parents, policymakers, and tech companies in promoting digital citizenship. Tech companies can contribute by creating safer and more child-friendly digital environments, as well as providing resources for digital wellness education.

As we strive to create a future where technology and mindful living coexist harmoniously, fostering digital citizenship in our future generations becomes paramount. The rise of tech-free zones and the growing movement towards mindful living in the digital age are steps in the right direction. By empowering our future generations with the principles of digital citizenship, we can prepare them for a future where they are not just consumers of technology, but responsible and mindful digital citizens.

The Harmonious Intersection of Technology and Mindfulness: A Vision for the Future

As we move further into the digital age, the intersection of technology and mindfulness emerges as a crucial theme in our collective narrative. As paradoxical as it may seem, the marriage of these two concepts is not only possible but essential for the future we want to shape. So, what might this future look like? Let's envision it together.

A Future Rooted in Balance

The crux of our future vision lies in balance. A future where technology and mindfulness coexist is one where we've mastered the art of digital balance. It is a future where technology doesn't overpower us but empowers us. It's a future where we've learned to control our tech habits rather than being controlled by them.

Imagine a day in this future. You wake up to a gentle alarm, not a flood of notifications. You enjoy your morning coffee without the compulsion to scroll through your social feed. Your workday is productive, free of unnecessary digital distractions. You have the tools and knowledge to use technology mindfully, in a way that enhances your life without overpowering it.

The Role of Tech-Free Zones

In this future, tech-free zones have become a norm. Homes, schools, workplaces, and public spaces have designated areas where devices are off-limits, creating pockets of peace in our bustling lives. These spaces are appreciated and respected, and their benefits are widely recognized. They represent our commitment to nurturing our mental, physical, and social well-being amidst the digital hustle.

The Contribution of Tech Companies

Tech companies play a significant role in shaping this future. They design products with digital wellness in mind, integrating features that encourage mindful use and discourage excessive screen time. Transparency is a norm, not an exception. Companies are candid about their algorithms, allowing users to make informed decisions about their tech use.

Empowered Future Generations

Our future generations grow up as proficient digital citizens. They are tech-savvy, yes, but they are also tech-wise. They understand the implications of their digital behaviors and know how to navigate the digital world responsibly. Schools educate students about digital wellness, teaching them the importance of tech-life balance from a young age.

Technology that Fosters Mindfulness

Mindfulness itself is leveraged by technology. A host of digital tools exist that encourage mindfulness and mental well-being - from apps that guide you through meditations to features that help manage screen time effectively. These tools help people incorporate mindfulness into their everyday lives, making it more accessible and achievable.

The Social Shift

Lastly, this harmonious future is characterized by a social shift - a change in our collective mindset. We are a society that values connection - real, human connection - as much as we value connectivity. We recognize the importance of being present in the moment, of engaging with the world around us without the filter of a screen.

In essence, the future we envision is one where technology and mindfulness are not at odds but in harmony. It's a future where we appreciate technology for its advantages while also recognizing the importance of stepping away from it. It's a future where we're not just surviving the digital age, but thriving in it.

And as we strive towards this future, each step we take, from setting up a tech-free corner in our homes to engaging in a digital wellness conversation, brings us closer to the harmonious intersection of technology and mindfulness. It's a journey, and every journey begins with a single step. So let's step forward, towards a future of digital balance, mindful living, and harmonious coexistence.

Chapter 9: Resources for Mindful Living and Digital Detox

Books, Blogs, Podcasts, and Courses

Welcome to the treasure trove of mindful living and digital detox resources. We're going to delve into the world of books, blogs, and podcasts that can serve as your guides as you embark on your digital detox journey. But remember, the most important resource of all is the one you're already utilizing—your commitment and determination to create a healthier relationship with technology.

Books

In a delicious twist of irony, one of the most effective tools to help with digital detoxification is something as decidedly analog as a good old-fashioned book. The tactile sensation of turning a page, the crisp aroma of the paper, the sound of a spine crackling—these are all sensory experiences that you may have overlooked in your digital lives. Now's the time to revisit and revel in them. Here are a few books that not only discuss the importance of detoxing from technology, but also offer practical strategies to do so:

1. **"Digital Minimalism: Choosing a Focused Life in a Noisy World" by Cal Newport.** This

thought-provoking book encourages readers to be more intentional with their use of technology, allowing them to create space for solitude and reflection. Newport presents a philosophical approach towards technology use, advocating for 'less is more'.

2. **"The Shallows: What the Internet Is Doing to Our Brains" by Nicholas Carr.** A somewhat alarming, yet enlightening read, Carr explores the implications of the Internet on our cognitive abilities. Reading it may make you reconsider how much time you spend online.

3. **"The Joy of Missing Out: Live More by Doing Less" by Tonya Dalton.** Dalton's book is all about embracing the concept of 'JOMO' and focusing on the quality rather than the quantity of our activities.

Blogs

If you're looking for short reads, real-time experiences, or the chance to interact with a community of like-minded individuals, blogs can be a wonderful resource. Here are a few that focus on mindful living, digital detox, and tech-life balance:

1. **Zen Habits by Leo Babauta.** This blog focuses on simplicity and mindfulness in the day-to-day life. The practical tips and relatable writing style make this blog an excellent resource for anyone looking to create a more mindful lifestyle.

2. **Be More With Less by Courtney Carver.** Through her personal experiences, Carver provides insights into how you can simplify your life, which includes decreasing your digital dependence.

3. **The Minimalists.** Started by Joshua Fields Millburn and Ryan Nicodemus, this blog explores the concept of living a meaningful life with less, including lesser digital clutter.

Podcasts

Listening to podcasts can be a great way to absorb new information while going about your day. If you want to be inspired, informed, and entertained on your digital detox journey, these podcasts are worth tuning into:

1. **"The Minimalists Podcast".** Joshua Fields Millburn and Ryan Nicodemus further expand their discussions on minimalism in this podcast, often tackling digital detox and mindful living topics.

2. **"Hurry Slowly" by Jocelyn K. Glei.** This podcast focuses on how you can be more productive, creative, and resilient through the simple act of slowing down.

3. **"Untangle" by Meditation Studio.** This podcast explores the stories of mindfulness leaders and how meditation has changed their lives, offering practical tips on incorporating mindfulness into your routine.

Online Courses

Although it may seem counterintuitive to recommend digital resources in a book about digital detox, remember that technology is not the villain here—it's our unbalanced relationship with it that we need to address. Some online platforms offer wonderful courses on mindful living and digital detox that are worth considering:

1. **Coursera: "The Science of Well-Being" by Yale University.** This course, delivered by Professor Laurie Santos, focuses on increasing happiness and building more productive habits, which includes managing our technology use.
2. **Udemy: "Digital Detox: Reset Your Mind & Business for Success."** This course targets professionals who want to declutter their digital life for enhanced productivity and work-life balance.
3. **MasterClass: "Headspace Co-Founder Andy Puddicombe Teaches Mindfulness and Meditation."** This class is an excellent introduction to mindfulness and how it can be used to navigate digital distractions.

These resources aren't magic spells that will instantly erase your digital dependencies. They're tools that, combined with your commitment and consistency, can assist you on your path to a balanced digital life.

Remember, while these resources can provide guidance and inspiration, the success of your digital detox journey ultimately depends on your actions. It's about implementing the strategies that resonate with you, and adapting them to your lifestyle.

Mindfulness Apps That Support Digital Detox

The marriage of technology and mindfulness might sound paradoxical at first. You might think, "Aren't we trying to escape digital devices?" Yes, that's true to some extent. But think of it this way: we're trying to reshape our relationship with technology, not divorce it entirely. There are a host of mindful apps designed to support your digital detox journey, and they can be incredibly useful. Let's explore some of the best ones out there.

"Headspace": Perhaps the most renowned mindfulness app, Headspace is an excellent starting point for your digital detox journey. It offers guided meditations, mindfulness exercises, and sleep resources designed by experts. Headspace aims to help you reduce stress, improve focus, and cultivate a sense of calm - the ideal state of mind to start a digital detox.

"Calm": Another popular mindfulness app, Calm offers a range of features from guided meditations and sleep stories to breathing exercises and stretching routines. With a primary focus on reducing stress and improving sleep, it's a fantastic resource for those looking to build mindful habits amidst digital overload.

"Forest: Stay Focused": Forest is a unique app that blends productivity and mindfulness. The concept is simple yet engaging: you plant a virtual seed in the app, which gradually grows into a tree. However, if you exit the app to use other digital distractions, your tree will wither and die. Forest gives you a visual incentive to stay focused and avoid digital distractions.

"Digital Detox": Digital Detox challenges you to quit smartphone addiction by embarking on game-like challenges. The app gives you the motivation to reduce smartphone usage and ultimately find a balance between your digital and real life.

"Moment": Moment tracks your device usage and provides insights on how much time you spend on different apps. It nudges you with reminders when you exceed your self-set limits and even offers short daily exercises based on your usage.

"Freedom": This app is a powerful tool to block distracting websites and apps across all your devices. With Freedom, you can schedule focused sessions during which you won't be able to access the digital distractions that you've chosen to block.

"Insight Timer": It offers more than 70,000 free meditations from mindfulness experts, neuroscientists, psychologists, and seasoned meditation practitioners. It's an ideal tool for cultivating mindfulness, managing stress, and improving sleep.

These apps serve as digital aids, helping you to cultivate mindfulness and reduce reliance on technology. However, remember that apps are merely tools. Their effectiveness largely depends on your willingness and commitment to change your habits. So, use them wisely, and they can be an excellent support system for your digital detox journey.

The key here is moderation. If you find yourself swapping one digital addiction for another, even if it's a mindfulness app, it may be time to reassess. The goal is to achieve a balanced, healthy relationship with technology where you're in control, not the device. With the right mindset, commitment, and resources, you'll be well on your way to a mindful, digitally balanced life.

Courses and Retreats

Sometimes, it takes more than self-guided learning and apps to truly break free from the digital chains that bind us. For those looking to deeply immerse themselves in the art of mindful living and digital detox, formal courses and retreats provide a structured and immersive experience.

Courses are often designed by experts who understand the nuances of our relationship with technology and can guide us through our detox journey effectively. Retreats, on the other hand, offer an escape from our everyday environments and routines, providing a tranquil space conducive to self-reflection and growth.

Let's explore some notable options:

"Digital Detox & Mindfulness Meditation Retreat": Hosted by various organizations worldwide, these retreats offer a unique blend of digital detox and mindfulness practice. They encourage guests to disconnect from their devices and reconnect with themselves and the world around them through meditation, yoga, and outdoor activities. The retreats are typically located in serene, natural environments, further promoting a sense of peace and calm.

"Center for Humane Technology's 'Your Undivided Attention' Course": This course was developed by the Center for Humane Technology, a team of ex-tech insiders passionate about realigning technology with humanity's best interests. The course provides a deep dive into the mechanics of attention economy, nudging you to rethink your relationship with technology.

"Digital Mindfulness Course by FutureLearn": This is a free online course that explores the concept of digital wellbeing. It offers a comprehensive look into the impact of digital technology on our mental health and provides strategies for achieving digital balance.

"Tech-Life Balance Bootcamp by Digital Mindfulness": A comprehensive six-week program that helps you establish healthy digital habits. It combines cognitive-behavioral strategies, mindfulness practices, and digital wellness principles to help you reduce digital overload.

"Unplug Meditation Studio Courses": This Los Angeles-based studio offers a variety of mindfulness and meditation courses, both online and in-person. Courses cover a range of topics, including managing stress, promoting sleep, and improving focus – all integral to a successful digital detox.

"Silent Meditation Retreats": Various organizations offer silent meditation retreats, which, while not directly focused on digital detox, provide a unique opportunity to disconnect from the digital world. The silence encourages deep introspection and mindfulness.

In essence, these courses and retreats can act as a catalyst for your digital detox journey, providing the tools, knowledge, and environment to foster a healthier relationship with technology.

While these programs offer a structured approach, it's important to remember that the ultimate goal is to integrate what you learn into your everyday life. The real success lies in maintaining a balanced, mindful lifestyle even after you return from a retreat or complete a course. It's about long-term change, not just a temporary respite.

Moreover, the options I've mentioned are just a start. Depending on your location, availability, and preference, you might find other courses or retreats more suitable. The most crucial factor is your commitment to the process. With dedication and an open mind, you're well-equipped to navigate this journey towards mindful living and digital detox.

Online Communities and Support Groups

In the journey of mindful living and digital detox, companionship can be a significant boon. Often, the shared experiences, wisdom, and encouragement found within online communities and support groups can make the path less daunting. It's reassuring to know that others are facing the same challenges, and their success stories can inspire your own.

Despite being digital, these platforms can play a vital role in your detox journey, offering a space to share experiences, seek advice, or simply connect with like-minded individuals. Here are some notable online communities and support groups:

"r/nosurf": This is a Reddit community dedicated to reducing internet use and promoting healthier digital habits. It's a lively forum where members share their experiences, tips, and strategies related to digital detox and mindful living. It's a supportive community that understands the struggles of internet addiction and promotes healthier usage.

"Time Well Spent": An initiative by the Center for Humane Technology, Time Well Spent is an online community aimed at reversing the digital attention crisis. It's a place where members discuss ideas and strategies to reclaim their time from digital distractions.

"Digital Detox Facebook Group": This group is an active community that shares tips, ideas, and personal experiences related to digital detox. The group also holds regular challenges to motivate members in their digital detox journey.

"Mindful Tech Community": This online community is dedicated to promoting mindful use of technology. It's a space to discuss ideas, share resources, and support each other in the journey towards digital mindfulness.

"Common Sense Media Community": Common Sense Media is an organization dedicated to promoting safe technology and media for children. Their community forum allows parents and educators to discuss the impact of digital media on kids and share strategies to manage it effectively.

"Break the Twitch Community": Based on the blog of the same name, this community focuses on intentional living in the digital age. Members discuss topics like minimalism, habits, and digital detox.

These communities and support groups can serve as a valuable part of your digital detox toolkit. However, remember to approach them mindfully. Use them for support and resources, but be wary of spending excessive time online, even if it's in a digital detox community.

Keep in mind that your journey is unique, and while advice and support can be valuable, your path may not look exactly like someone else's. Use these communities to inspire and guide your journey, but always listen to your own intuition and needs.

You're the captain of your digital detox ship, and these communities are your supportive crew. Together, you're setting sail towards the calm shores of mindful living in the digital age.

Chapter 10: Interviews and Case Studies: Real-Life Experiences with Tech Detox

Life before and After Tech Detox: Personal Stories

Digital technology has permeated our everyday lives in ways both discernible and subtle. On one hand, we have the tangible – the devices we hold, the screens we stare at, and the sounds we listen to. On the other, we have the intangible – the constant flow of information, the invisible ties of social networks, and the unending pull of digital dopamine. With this omnipresence of technology, a counter movement has arisen, a movement committed to living mindfully in the digital age: the tech detox.

In this chapter, we're going to take a closer look at the experiences of individuals who've undergone this journey. Through interviews and personal narratives, we'll uncover their motivations, challenges, triumphs, and the lasting impact of their tech detox journey. We'll follow their transformation, from the moment they felt the need to disconnect, to the new habits and perceptions they've adopted in their digitally-detoxed lives.

Case Study 1: The Overwhelmed Entrepreneur

Meet John, a successful tech entrepreneur in his mid-thirties. His life, prior to the detox, was a whirlwind of business meetings, emails, notifications, and social media interactions. "I was always plugged in," John recalls. "I would wake up to emails and go to bed to the glow of my laptop screen. I realized I was never truly present in my own life."

Driven by a gnawing feeling of digital overwhelm and exhaustion, John embarked on a month-long tech detox. This meant no emails, social media, or digital entertainment. The initial week was a struggle. "It was like a phantom limb syndrome. I'd constantly reach for my phone, expecting it to be there. But it wasn't."

As the weeks progressed, John started noticing changes. "My mind felt less cluttered. I started engaging more deeply in conversations, noticing things around me I'd ignored before. I read more books in that month than I had in the last two years." Post-detox, John implemented strict boundaries on his tech use, dedicating specific 'offline' periods each day. "It's given me back control over my time and attention."

Case Study 2: The Social Media Enthusiast

Sandra, a 28-year-old social media enthusiast, confesses she used to spend nearly every waking moment on various platforms, endlessly scrolling, posting, and commenting. "It was a vicious cycle," she admits, "My self-worth began to be tied to likes and comments. I constantly compared myself to others and always felt inadequate."

Sandra's tech detox journey began when she realized she was losing hours to her screen each day. She started small, limiting her social media use to certain times, then eventually went for a full week-long detox.

"That week was enlightening," Sandra says, "I had time. Actual time to spend with friends, read, and pursue hobbies." The experience changed Sandra's relationship with social media. Now, she sets limits on her screen time, focusing more on real-life interactions. "I still use social media, but I'm not a slave to it anymore. I've realized that real-life is happening outside the screen."

Case Study 3: The Digital Artist

Our next story comes from Amy, a 32-year-old digital artist. In her profession, constant exposure to digital platforms is a requirement. "I was working on my computer, promoting myself on social media, learning new techniques through online tutorials...it was all happening in the same space, my screen."

Amy noticed the impact when she started experiencing digital eye strain and a general feeling of burnout. "I felt trapped," she admits. "I love my job, but the constant exposure was exhausting."

The idea of a tech detox was daunting at first due to her work requirements, but Amy decided to approach it creatively. She initiated 'tech-free' Sundays, when she would explore traditional art forms like sketching, painting, or pottery. "I was amazed at how much I had missed working with my hands, feeling the texture of the material," she shares.

Post-detox, Amy maintains tech-free Sundays and has further adopted the practice of taking regular screen breaks during her workdays. "It's a balance," she says. "We can't escape technology, especially in my line of work. But we can certainly find ways to manage it better."

Case Study 4: The Always-Connected Student

Meet Mark, a 21-year-old university student. His life was a constant juggling act between online classes, assignments, group chats, and digital entertainment. "I was always connected, either for academics or recreation. My screen was the first thing I saw in the morning and the last thing I saw at night."

Mark's turning point was when he realized he was having trouble sleeping and was often anxious. "I was always anticipating the next email or message, even when I was trying to rest," he admits.

He decided to try a tech detox during a spring break. The first two days, as he puts it, were "uncomfortable." But then things started to change. "I started sleeping better, I felt less anxious, and I started doing things I always said I didn't have time for – like reading for pleasure and learning to play the guitar."

Post-detox, Mark has developed new habits to balance his screen time. He has implemented 'no screens' rule two hours before bedtime and regularly practices digital sabbaticals. "It's not easy," he admits, "But it's necessary. We need to take charge of our tech use, instead of letting it control us."

Case Study 5: The Remote Worker

Let's talk about Laura, a 36-year-old remote worker for an international company. Her job involves handling customer support, managing emails, attending virtual meetings, and often working across different time zones. "I was always 'on,' even during my off-hours," Laura reflects. "It was so easy to just open my laptop and start working or respond to an email at all hours."

Laura began to experience chronic headaches, sleep disturbances, and a creeping sense of social isolation. This prompted her to consider a tech detox. For a full week, she took time off work and unplugged completely. "I was scared at first. I thought, 'what if they need me?' But I knew this was something I had to do for my wellbeing."

The detox period was an eye-opener. "I had forgotten what it was like to live without constantly checking my devices," Laura shares. She found time to reconnect with nature, picking up hiking and bird-watching. "It was peaceful. I had forgotten what that peace felt like."

Now, Laura has set strict boundaries between her work and personal life. She has dedicated work hours and ensures she is offline during her personal time. "I have regained my peace and can concentrate better at work. The detox helped me to reset and rebuild healthier habits."

Case Study 6: The Tech-Savvy Senior

Lastly, we have David, a 67-year-old retired teacher who had enthusiastically adopted technology as a means to stay connected with family, read the news, and pursue online learning. But over time, David found himself spending more and more time online. "It was consuming me. I was always exploring something new, learning a new tool, or chatting," he said.

David's tech detox involved replacing screen time with physical activities, book reading, and more face-to-face socializing. "The tech detox wasn't as hard as I thought it would be. I had been around before this technology explosion, so I just had to remind myself of life before the digital."

The detox led David to discover a more balanced relationship with technology. He set up specific hours for using digital devices and chose to spend more time in his garden, joining a local book club, and volunteering at community centers. "Tech has its place, but it's not the be-all and end-all. There's more to life, and the detox reminded me of that."

Through the lens of these case studies, we witness a shared journey towards balancing technology use and personal well-being. These individuals represent different ages, professions, and lifestyles, yet their stories converge on the shared benefits of a tech detox: increased presence, richer offline experiences, improved mental health, and a regained sense of control over their digital lives.

As varied as these stories are, they share a common thread: the realization that their relationship with technology was becoming unhealthy, the courage to make a change, and the rewards they reaped by doing so. In their own ways, each has found a path to a more mindful existence in our digital world, showing us that it is indeed possible.

Beyond the Western World: Global Perspectives on Tech Detox and Mindful Living

So far, we have primarily discussed the concept of tech detox within a Western context. However, the global digital revolution has impacted societies across the world, each with their unique cultural nuances and strategies for managing technology's influence. In this section, we will take a journey beyond the Western world to explore how different cultures approach tech detox and mindful living in the digital age.

Japan - The Art of 'Digital Minimalism'

In Japan, the principle of 'ma' or 'space' influences many aspects of life, from art and design to social interactions. This principle is also applied in their approach to technology. "In Japan, we believe in balance and moderation," shares Hiroshi, a tech entrepreneur from Tokyo. "We understand the benefits of technology, but we also respect the space between us and our devices."

Digital minimalism in Japan goes beyond tech detox. It is a lifestyle choice that promotes a more mindful and deliberate use of technology. It involves creating a physical and mental 'space' from digital devices, reducing unnecessary digital clutter, and focusing on quality over quantity in digital interactions.

India - Yoga and Mindfulness in the Digital Age

In India, traditional practices like yoga and meditation are often used as tools to manage the stress of the digital age. "Yoga is not just about physical exercises," explains Priya, a yoga teacher from Bangalore. "It's a holistic approach to wellbeing that includes managing our relationship with external influences, including technology."

Tech detox retreats are popular in India, where participants can unplug from technology and engage in yoga, meditation, and nature walks. These retreats are often seen not as a complete escape from technology, but as a way to reset and cultivate a more mindful approach to digital usage.

South Africa - Ubuntu and Community-Based Approach to Tech Detox

In South Africa, the philosophy of Ubuntu, emphasizing community and interconnectedness, influences the approach to tech detox. "Ubuntu teaches us that our wellbeing is interconnected," says Thulani, a community leader in Johannesburg. "If one of us is struggling with technology overuse, it impacts the community."

In response, community-based tech detox programs have been initiated, where members collectively decide to limit their tech use for certain periods. "It's a collective effort," Thulani says. "We are there to support and encourage each other, reminding ourselves that there's more to life than what's on our screens."

Australia - Indigenous Perspectives on Tech Detox and Connection to Nature

In Australia, some indigenous communities are using their deep connection with nature as a tool for tech detox. "Our ancestors have always known the importance of connection with the land," shares Kaya, an indigenous health worker. "We try to incorporate this knowledge in dealing with the challenges of the digital age."

Tech detox in these communities often involves spending time in nature without digital distractions, allowing individuals to reconnect with their surroundings and themselves. "It's about remembering our roots and grounding ourselves in the natural world, which is often lost in digital interactions," says Kaya.

These global perspectives highlight the diversity of approaches to tech detox and mindful living in the digital age. While the strategies may vary, the underlying principles remain similar: balance, moderation, mindfulness, community, and reconnection with the self and the natural world.

These universal themes underscore the shared human experience in navigating our relationship with technology, reinforcing that we are not alone in this journey, no matter where we are in the world.

Chapter 11: Mindful Parenting in the Digital Age

Recognizing the Unique Challenges of Digital Age Parenting

As we step into this new chapter, we find ourselves faced with an essential, yet often overlooked, facet of our digital lives - parenting in the digital age. Becoming a mindful digital parent is about much more than setting boundaries and monitoring screen time; it's about navigating the unique challenges of raising children in a world that's more connected and yet, paradoxically, more isolated than ever before.

First, let's acknowledge that the terrain of the digital age is unfamiliar and evolving. This generation of parents is the first to raise children who are 'digital natives,' a term coined by Marc Prensky in 2001 to describe individuals born into an inherently digital world. The digital landscape today's children inhabit is richly diverse, spanning everything from educational platforms to online gaming communities, from social media networks to creative hubs like YouTube or TikTok.

This broad digital ecosystem offers incredible opportunities for learning, creativity, and connection. But, as we well know, it also presents unique challenges and potential dangers. Cyberbullying, online predators, data privacy concerns, and the impact of screen time on physical and mental health are just a few of the issues digital age parents must navigate.

A key challenge here is the gap in tech-savviness between parents and their children. With technology evolving at a rapid pace, it can feel as though our children are speaking a different language - a language of memes, hashtags, and emojis, filled with shifting online trends and fads. As parents, we may struggle to understand this language, let alone guide our children in using it responsibly.

Then there's the question of balance. With so much of modern life happening online - from schoolwork to socializing - it's not realistic (or necessarily healthy) to simply ban screens altogether. So, how do we find a middle ground? How do we encourage our children to engage with the digital world in a balanced, mindful way that enhances rather than diminishes their well-being?

The phenomenon of 'sharenting' - the practice of sharing aspects of our children's lives on social media - also poses unique ethical and privacy concerns. What are the implications of creating a digital footprint for our children before they're old enough to consent? And how do we navigate the social pressures of parenting in an age where every milestone is often shared – and scrutinized – online?

Digital age parenting also involves teaching our children critical digital literacy skills. In an era of fake news and information overload, it's crucial that we empower our children to think critically, to question the sources of their information, and to understand the algorithms that shape what they see online.

Then there's the challenge of role modeling. Our children learn from us, so how we use technology matters just as much, if not more, than the rules we set. It's not enough to preach the virtues of screen-free time if we're glued to our smartphones. Mindful digital parenting involves embodying the values and behaviors we want our children to adopt.

Indeed, the challenges of digital age parenting are manifold and complex, requiring us to navigate uncharted territory. But as we'll see in the coming chapters, they're also surmountable. By fostering open communication, teaching digital literacy, modeling balanced tech use, and setting clear boundaries, we can raise children who are not just savvy navigators of the digital world, but thoughtful, responsible digital citizens.

As we venture deeper into the chapter, let's dissect some of these challenges further, providing insights and practical tips to address them.

1. Navigating the Tech-Savvy Gap

The tech-savvy gap can be daunting. It's essential to remember that it's not about mastering every new app or platform your child uses, but understanding the risks and benefits these platforms present. Spend time with your children as they engage with technology. Ask them to show you how they use their favorite apps, what they love about them, and what worries them. This not only aids you in understanding their digital world but also opens up lines of communication, reinforcing that you're a trusted source of guidance.

2. Striking a Balance with Screen Time

Setting boundaries around screen time is a tricky endeavor. Rather than enforcing a one-size-fits-all rule, consider your child's individual needs and the nature of their screen use. Is it for schoolwork, connecting with friends, or creative expression? Is it interfering with sleep, physical activity, or face-to-face interaction? Use these questions as a guide to create a balanced digital diet that suits your child's developmental needs and lifestyle.

3. Navigating the Perils of 'Sharenting'

Sharing our children's lives on social media can be a minefield. It's crucial to seek your child's consent before posting about them, where age-appropriate, and to regularly review your privacy settings. Be mindful of the details you share and remember that once something is online, it's challenging to completely remove. Consider creating a separate, private channel (like a group chat or email thread) for sharing updates with close family and friends.

4. **Cultivating Digital Literacy**

Help your children understand the mechanics behind the digital world. Explain how algorithms work, teach them to differentiate between reliable and unreliable sources of information, and encourage them to question the motives behind the content they consume. Equip them with the tools they need to become informed, critical consumers of digital content.

5. **Role Modeling Healthy Tech Habits**

Your digital habits significantly influence your children's behavior. Therefore, it's crucial to embody the mindful tech habits you'd like them to adopt. Regularly disconnect from devices, especially during family time, to show the importance of in-person interaction. Share your own struggles and successes in navigating the digital world, fostering a family culture of openness and mutual support around technology use.

The digital age presents new frontiers in parenting that can seem overwhelming. But, with mindfulness and open dialogue, we can guide our children to navigate this landscape responsibly and reap the benefits of this connected world.

The goal isn't to shield our children from the digital world completely, but to prepare them to engage with it in a thoughtful, balanced, and ethical way.

As we continue exploring this topic in subsequent chapters, we'll delve deeper into practical strategies for achieving this goal, focusing on specific areas like managing screen time, promoting digital safety, and fostering digital citizenship.

Together, we can chart a course through the digital landscape that equips our children with the skills, understanding, and resilience they need to thrive in the digital age.

Strategies for Promoting Mindful Screen Time for Children

Finding a balance in screen time for children is not about being overly strict or exceedingly lenient but involves a careful, mindful approach that both recognizes the importance of technology and respects the limits of healthy consumption. Here are some thoughtful strategies that could guide you in this process:

1. Establish Screen-Free Zones and Times:

Creating designated areas and times in your home that are free of screens can instill the value of disconnection. This could be the dinner table or the bedroom, reinforcing the importance of meals and sleep without distractions. Consider setting aside 'tech-free' times, such as the first hour after coming home from school, to encourage other activities.

2. Encourage Active Screen Time:

Not all screen time is created equal. There's a significant difference between passive consumption and active engagement. Encourage activities that promote creativity, problem-solving, and active learning, such as coding apps, digital art platforms, and educational games. This transforms screen time into a more enriching experience.

3. Discuss and Set Boundaries Together:

Involving children in discussions about screen time rules makes it more likely they will understand and respect these boundaries. Talk about the reasoning behind the limits, the potential consequences of excessive screen use, and negotiate terms that feel fair to everyone. This fosters a sense of responsibility and autonomy in your child's digital habits.

4. Use Tech Tools Mindfully:

Make use of the tools many digital platforms offer to monitor and limit screen time. This can help children develop an awareness of their usage patterns. However, these should be used as guides, not substitutes for open dialogue and mutual understanding.

5. **Encourage Alternative Activities:**

Children are less likely to overuse screens if they have plenty of other engaging activities. Encourage hobbies that require movement, foster creativity, and facilitate social interaction. This could be anything from sports and art to board games and family outings.

6. **Be a Role Model:**

Children mimic adult behavior, so be aware of your own screen habits. Try to show a balanced digital lifestyle that includes tech-free activities. When you do use technology, let it be for meaningful activities and demonstrate active, not just passive, engagement.

These strategies aren't about enforcing strict rules, but guiding your children towards a more mindful engagement with technology.

As stated previously, the goal is not to eliminate screen time, but to make that time count for something valuable and ensure it doesn't overshadow other important areas of life. It's a collaborative journey that requires understanding, communication, and mutual respect.

Role Modeling Mindful Digital Habits: Parents as Pioneers

As parents, our role extends beyond just establishing boundaries and monitoring our children's digital habits. We are, in essence, pioneers – the trailblazers they look up to as they navigate their digital journey. If we want our children to adopt mindful digital habits, we need to model these behaviors ourselves. We can't underestimate the power of leading by example. Let's explore how we can incorporate this into our daily lives.

1. **Demonstrate Balanced Use of Technology:**

One of the most significant ways you can model mindful tech habits is by demonstrating a balanced approach to your own device use. Show your children that while technology plays an essential role in our lives, it's not the be-all and end-all. Make a conscious effort to set aside your devices during family time, meals, and other key moments. Show them that while our devices are valuable tools, they're just that - tools, not the center of our lives.

2. **Make Your Digital Activities Visible and Discuss Them:**

Often, children see parents on their devices but have no idea what they're doing. Are you working? Reading news?

Scrolling through social media? When appropriate, share with your children what you're doing and why. This visibility can help them understand that screens have various uses, not just entertainment.

3. **Show How You Manage Digital Distractions:**

How do you react when you get a notification during a conversation? Do you immediately check your phone every time it buzzes? Model how to manage these digital interruptions. Show your children how you put your device on "Do Not Disturb" mode during family time or how you set aside specific times to check emails and messages.

4. **Share Your Own Challenges and Solutions:**

Let your children know that managing digital distractions and maintaining balance isn't always easy, even for adults. Share your struggles, your mistakes, and how you're trying to address them. This openness can make you more approachable and relatable, encouraging your children to share their digital challenges with you.

5. **Model Digital Kindness and Responsibility:**

Your online behavior can set the tone for your children's digital etiquette. Model respectful and kind communication in your digital interactions. Similarly, demonstrate responsibility by respecting people's privacy online and not sharing everything on social media. Show them that the principles of respect and kindness apply online as they do offline.

6. Teach Through Your Actions:

Your approach to technology can directly inform your children's understanding of its value. Show them through your actions that technology is a tool that can be used creatively, productively, and responsibly, rather than a means of passive consumption.

By pioneering mindful digital habits, parents can guide their children towards a healthier, more mindful relationship with technology. The essence of this endeavor lies in being the change you wish to see in your children's digital habits.

In this way, you equip them not only with rules to follow but also with values to live by in the digital age. It's a significant responsibility, no doubt, but it's also an incredible opportunity to shape the digital citizens of tomorrow.

New Findings: The Impact of Parental Tech Habits on Child Development

As we navigate the terrain of digital age parenting, it's crucial to keep abreast of the latest research in the field. Our understanding of how parental tech habits impact child development is continually evolving, reflecting the dynamic nature of the digital world. Let's explore some recent findings that shed light on this critical issue.

1. **Tech-Imposed Parental Absence:**

Research increasingly highlights the concept of 'technoference,' where daily interactions are interrupted by digital and mobile technology. Studies suggest that parental screen use can lead to 'absent presence'— a state where the parent is physically present but mentally distracted. This can result in decreased parent-child interactions, which are essential for a child's social and emotional development. It's a powerful reminder of the importance of being fully present and engaged during our interactions with our children.

2. **Modeling Screen Habits:**

Multiple studies suggest that children often model their screen habits on their parents'. A parent who is often on their device is likely to have children who spend significant amounts of time on screens. In contrast, parents who demonstrate balanced tech use — setting aside time for device-free activities and mindful screen use — often see these habits reflected in their children.

3. **The Effect on Physical Health:**

Parental screen use has also been linked to children's physical health. One study found a correlation between the amount of time parents spend on devices and the likelihood of increased screen time in children, leading to sedentary behavior. This sedentary behavior is associated with a higher risk of obesity and other health problems in children.

4. Impact on Parent-Child Relationships:

Some research indicates that excessive parental screen use can strain parent-child relationships. Children can feel unimportant or ignored when their parents are constantly 'plugged in', leading to feelings of frustration and even behavioral issues.

5. Influence on Sleep Habits:

Parents' tech habits can also influence children's sleep patterns. Using screens close to bedtime is known to interfere with the quality of sleep due to the blue light emitted by devices.

When children see their parents using screens late into the night, they are more likely to adopt similar habits, affecting their sleep hygiene.

These findings underscore the significant impact our digital habits can have on our children's development. They serve as a reminder that as parents, we need to not only monitor our children's screen use but also be mindful of our own.

Being aware of this research can help us make informed decisions about our tech use and foster a family environment where technology is used mindfully and in a balanced way.

Remember, the goal isn't perfection but progress. Each step we take towards more mindful tech use is a step towards healthier digital habits for our entire family.

Chapter 12: Mindful Tech in Education

The Role of Technology in Modern Education: A Double-Edged Sword

The ever-present hum of technology in our lives is as familiar as the steady heartbeat we experience from moment to moment. This reality is no different in the field of education. The past few decades have seen an explosion of technological advancements that have significantly altered our approach to learning and teaching. Our classrooms have morphed from chalk and blackboard to smart boards and virtual reality, transforming the education landscape at an unprecedented pace. However, just like any other aspect of life, the intersection of education and technology is a double-edged sword.

To appreciate this dual nature of technology in education, we first need to acknowledge the significant benefits it has bestowed upon us. It has the ability to transcend geographical boundaries, democratize access to knowledge, personalize learning experiences, and ignite curiosity and creativity like never before. With the advent of the internet and digital technologies, the acquisition of knowledge is no longer bound by the four walls of a classroom or the availability of a local library. An enthusiastic learner, anywhere in the world, can tap into a multitude of resources, explore online courses from prestigious universities, and engage in thought-provoking discussions with a global community.

Not only that, but technology has also offered innovative ways to cater to the diverse learning needs and paces of individual students. Adaptive learning platforms can provide personalized curriculums that adjust based on a student's performance. Simultaneously, gamified learning experiences can make education more engaging and fun, especially for younger students. Plus, the power of data analytics allows teachers and administrators to track students' progress and provide real-time feedback, ensuring that no student is left behind.

However, while these advantages are groundbreaking, they are not without their drawbacks. This is where the double-edged sword of technology in education becomes apparent. As we integrate more technology into our education systems, we're also inviting a host of potential issues - from digital addiction and reduced physical activity, to privacy concerns and socio-economic disparities in access to quality tech resources.

Just as it's crucial to keep in mind the enormous benefits of tech in education, it's equally important to be cognizant of the potential pitfalls. Schools, teachers, and parents need to ensure that technology is used mindfully and responsibly in the classroom and beyond. Unchecked screen time and digital distractions can lead to negative effects on students' physical health, social skills, and overall wellbeing. Additionally, while technology can make learning more engaging, it can also lead to information overload, stress, and anxiety.

Perhaps more seriously, the rapid shift towards digital learning has also highlighted an urgent issue - the digital divide. This is the gap between those who have easy access to computers and the internet, and those who do not. It's an issue that cuts across socio-economic lines and exacerbates educational disparities among students from different backgrounds. It's a challenge that must be addressed if we are to ensure that the benefits of tech in education are equitably distributed.

Moreover, data privacy is another significant concern. As more educational content moves online and learning becomes increasingly data-driven, the potential for misuse or mishandling of personal data rises. Protecting students' privacy and ensuring that their personal information is safe must be a top priority.

The role of technology in modern education, then, is a complex and multifaceted one. It holds the power to transform and elevate learning, yet, without mindful use and regulation, it can also introduce significant challenges. As we navigate this new era of digital education, we must strive to harness the positive aspects of technology, while minimizing and mitigating its potential drawbacks. Mindful tech in education is about striking this delicate balance, an equilibrium that respects the capabilities of tech without losing sight of the holistic development of students.

In the grand pursuit of this equilibrium, mindfulness plays a critical role. It involves intentionally directing our attention and awareness to the present moment, acknowledging our thoughts, feelings, and the surrounding environment without judgment. Applying mindfulness in the context of education technology requires the conscious use of digital tools, being aware of their impacts, and adapting our behaviors accordingly.

For students, it's about learning to use tech tools to enhance their educational experience, not detract from it. They must be educated on the responsible use of technology, understanding when it's beneficial to their learning and when it's a potential distraction. Educators and parents have an essential role in guiding students on this path, teaching them to strike a balance between online and offline activities, and helping them understand the value of screen-free time.

For teachers, mindful tech in education means judiciously incorporating digital tools into their teaching practice. It involves discerning which technologies genuinely enrich the learning process and which ones merely add a sheen of novelty without substantive benefits. Teachers should also strive to understand the nuances of their students' digital lives, empathizing with their challenges, and helping them navigate the often-overwhelming digital landscape.

For schools and policy makers, mindfulness in tech adoption involves scrutinizing how and where technology is integrated into the curriculum. They must ensure that the implementation of technology does not widen the gap in educational equity and that students' data privacy is uncompromised. Moreover, they should continuously evaluate the effectiveness and impact of the technology used in education to make necessary adjustments and refinements.

Finally, for tech companies and developers, mindful tech means designing and building products that respect the learner's attention, privacy, and time. They should strive for creating tools that truly enhance learning without adding unnecessary complexities or distractions.

The double-edged sword of technology in education should not deter us. Rather, it should remind us of the need for continuous mindfulness and thoughtful stewardship of our digital world. We must aim to create an educational environment where technology serves as a tool of empowerment, not of domination; a tool of opportunity, not of division.

Navigating this path won't be easy. It requires ongoing dialogues, research, education, and policy changes. But the potential rewards - a more equitable, engaging, and effective education system - are undoubtedly worth the efforts. Through mindfulness, we can wield the double-edged sword of technology in education to cut through barriers, rather than letting it cut us apart.

Incorporating Mindfulness Practices in Classroom Settings

Integrating technology into classrooms has provided an exciting new horizon for education, but it has also brought forth new challenges and considerations. One crucial aspect we've touched upon is the practice of mindfulness in the context of this digital revolution. Mindfulness, the art of paying attention in a particular way, on purpose, in the present moment, and nonjudgmentally, is key to using technology in a balanced and beneficial way. But how do we go about incorporating mindfulness practices in classroom settings?

First and foremost, it's essential to foster an overall mindfulness culture within the school environment. This involves making mindfulness a priority at all levels, from the students and teachers to the administration. Workshops, training sessions, and resources should be made available to everyone in the school community to introduce and normalize the concept of mindfulness. The goal is to cultivate an atmosphere where conscious and intentional use of technology is encouraged and rewarded.

One specific strategy is to start each class with a brief mindfulness exercise, whether it's a couple of minutes of quiet reflection or a short guided meditation. This practice helps students center themselves and prepare their minds for learning. It also encourages them to become more aware of their digital habits and how these habits affect their attention and focus. The idea is to create a calm, present, and engaged atmosphere conducive to effective learning, even in a tech-heavy environment.

Teachers can also integrate mindfulness techniques into the teaching of digital literacy and citizenship. For instance, during a lesson on internet use or social media, teachers can discuss the concept of mindful scrolling, where students are encouraged to pay attention to how they're feeling as they engage with digital content. Students can be taught to question why they're using certain apps or services, how these platforms make them feel, and whether they're using them out of habit or intention.

In addition, regular digital detox sessions can be a beneficial practice in the classroom. Designating specific times during the week for unplugging and focusing on non-tech activities can help students reset their digital habits and better understand their relationship with technology. These sessions can provide a safe space for students to reflect on their tech usage, discuss their experiences, and develop more mindful habits.

Moreover, teachers should strive to model mindful tech behavior themselves. After all, students often learn more from what they observe than from what they're told. If teachers are frequently distracted by their own devices or seem to rely heavily on tech for every aspect of teaching, students may adopt a similar approach. By contrast, if teachers show a balanced, intentional, and mindful use of technology, students are more likely to do the same.

Lastly, mindfulness should extend to how we design and choose the digital tools we incorporate into the classroom. Not all apps, platforms, or devices are created equal. It's crucial to select tools that truly enhance learning and respect students' attention and privacy. This involves critically evaluating a tool's features, understanding its potential drawbacks, and staying informed about the latest research and recommendations regarding ed-tech.

Incorporating mindfulness practices in classroom settings is an ongoing journey, not a one-time fix. It requires continuous effort, open dialogues, and a willingness to adapt and evolve. Yet, this effort is undoubtedly worthwhile. By fostering mindful tech habits, we're not just enhancing students' learning experiences - we're also equipping them with the skills and habits they need to navigate the digital age with resilience, balance, and intention.

Mindful EdTech: Emerging Trends and Tools

As we strive to incorporate mindfulness practices into the digital landscape of education, it's imperative to keep up with the latest trends and tools that facilitate this goal. In recent years, several mindful EdTech trends have emerged, and a plethora of tools have been developed to promote mindful learning in the digital realm. Let's delve into some of these developments.

Mindfulness and Wellbeing Apps

A significant trend in mindful EdTech is the rise of mindfulness and wellbeing apps specifically designed for educational settings. These apps are created to help students and teachers alike practice mindfulness, reduce stress, and cultivate emotional resilience. Applications like Headspace, Calm, and Smiling Mind offer guided meditations, breathing exercises, and mindful activities that can be used in the classroom or at home. They can be a valuable tool for starting a mindfulness practice or enhancing an existing one.

Digital Minimalism

Digital minimalism, another emerging trend, advocates for a more intentional and selective approach to tech use. It's about choosing quality over quantity when it comes to digital tools and platforms. In terms of EdTech, this could mean focusing on a few impactful tools that genuinely enhance learning, instead of overwhelming students and teachers with numerous apps and platforms. This trend not only simplifies the tech landscape but also encourages mindful and purposeful use of technology.

AI and Personalized Learning

Artificial Intelligence (AI) is rapidly advancing in the field of education. AI-powered platforms can adapt to a learner's individual pace and style, providing a personalized learning experience. However, the mindfulness angle is ensuring that these platforms are used to complement human instruction, not replace it. They should be used consciously and intentionally, with students and teachers both understanding their benefits and limitations.

Virtual and Augmented Reality (VR/AR)

VR and AR technologies are bringing immersive learning experiences to classrooms. These tools can stimulate students' curiosity and engagement in a unique and powerful way. Mindful usage here involves ensuring that these experiences do not overstimulate or distract students but genuinely add value to their learning process. It also involves balancing screen-based VR/AR activities with offline, real-world experiences.

Digital Citizenship Platforms

In an era where much of our lives are lived online, teaching students to be responsible digital citizens is crucial. Platforms like Common Sense Education offer resources to teach students about online safety, digital footprints, and respectful communication. The key to mindful use of these platforms is to integrate digital citizenship lessons into everyday learning and to ensure students understand why these skills are essential.

Privacy-focused EdTech

As we've discussed earlier, data privacy is a serious concern in the digital age. Thankfully, there's an increasing trend towards more privacy-focused EdTech tools. These platforms prioritize data encryption, anonymous usage, and transparent data policies to ensure students' personal information is safe. A mindful approach to choosing EdTech tools should always involve scrutinizing the tool's privacy policies and data handling practices.

Mindful Tech Training for Teachers

Finally, there's a growing recognition of the need for professional development opportunities focusing on mindful tech use for teachers. Several organizations now offer workshops, courses, and resources aimed at helping teachers navigate the digital education landscape with mindfulness and intention. Teachers are encouraged to participate in these opportunities to further their understanding and ability to integrate mindful practices into their classrooms.

By understanding these trends and being selective about the tools we use, we can leverage the power of technology to support mindful education. The goal isn't to reject technology but to use it in a way that respects our attention, values our privacy, and genuinely enhances the learning process. As the field of mindful EdTech continues to evolve, it's an exciting time to be part of the journey towards a more balanced and intentional digital education landscape.

Implications for Future Learning: A Balance Between Online and Offline Education

As we continue to forge our path in the digital education landscape, one thing becomes increasingly clear: the future of learning isn't about choosing between online or offline education—it's about striking a balance between the two. In the subsequent sections, we'll explore the implications of this balanced approach for future learning and how mindful practices can guide us towards this equilibrium.

Integrating Online and Offline Learning Experiences

The increased integration of technology in classrooms and the rise of online learning platforms have revolutionized education, offering increased accessibility and personalization. However, we must remember that technology is a tool to enhance education, not a replacement for traditional, offline learning experiences. The goal is to create a blended learning environment where online and offline activities complement each other.

For instance, technology can be used to provide interactive lessons, simulations, and virtual tours, bringing concepts to life in a way that traditional teaching methods might not. At the same time, offline activities, such as group discussions, hands-on experiments, and field trips, offer valuable opportunities for collaboration, physical engagement, and real-world application of knowledge. The key is to use each mode of learning where it shines best and to create a seamless, integrated experience for students.

The Importance of Screen-Free Time

While technology offers immense educational benefits, it's equally important to promote screen-free time. Extended screen time can lead to physical discomfort, reduced physical activity, and over-reliance on digital stimulation. Encouraging regular breaks from screens can help students reset, reduce stress, and foster a healthier relationship with technology.

Screen-free time can be incorporated into the school day in various ways, from outdoor play and sports to arts, music, and other non-tech based activities. Schools can also promote screen-free periods at home, such as implementing no-device rules during meal times or before bed. These practices not only balance tech use but also encourage students to engage in a variety of activities that promote holistic development.

Promoting Digital Wellbeing

As we blend online and offline education, promoting digital wellbeing becomes paramount. This involves teaching students to use technology responsibly and mindfully. Students should be educated about the potential risks of excessive or inappropriate tech use, such as cyberbullying, digital addiction, and invasion of privacy. They should also be taught strategies for managing these risks, such as setting boundaries for tech use, critically evaluating digital content, and safeguarding personal information.

Addressing the Digital Divide

A balanced approach to online and offline education also has implications for addressing the digital divide. While technology can democratize access to education, it can also exacerbate inequalities if not everyone has equal access to quality tech resources. Schools and policy makers need to work towards ensuring that all students, regardless of their socio-economic backgrounds, have the necessary tools and skills to benefit from digital education. This could involve investing in infrastructure, providing affordable or free devices and internet access, and offering digital literacy training to underserved communities.

Preparing Students for the Future

Finally, a balanced approach to online and offline education is crucial for preparing students for the future.

In the digital age, students need to be fluent in technology and digital tools. However, they also need to develop offline skills such as critical thinking, creativity, and interpersonal communication. By incorporating both online and offline learning experiences, we can equip students with a comprehensive skill set that prepares them for the future, whatever it may hold.

The future of learning is not about choosing between online or offline education but about balancing the two. With mindful practices at its core, this balanced approach can help us navigate the digital education landscape, leveraging the power of technology while ensuring holistic development and wellbeing of our students. It's a journey of continuous adaptation and learning, but one that holds the promise of shaping an education system that is dynamic, inclusive, and attuned to the realities and possibilities of the digital age.

In essence, the implications for future learning signal a shift in the way we perceive and interact with technology in the classroom. This shift requires everyone—students, educators, parents, policymakers, and technology developers—to work together in adopting a balanced, mindful approach to online and offline education.

To maintain this balance, we must treat technology as an aid, not a crutch; a means to an end, not the end in itself. We must continuously evaluate our digital practices, making adjustments when necessary, and ensure we are not compromising our physical and mental wellbeing in the process.

Moreover, we should leverage technology as a tool for fostering inclusivity, making sure every student has the opportunity to benefit from digital learning tools, while ensuring these tools don't create new barriers or widen existing gaps in education equity.

Ultimately, our goal is to cultivate a learning environment where technology supports students' holistic development, enhances their learning experience, and prepares them for a future that will undoubtedly be intertwined with digital advancements. A future where they feel empowered by technology, not overwhelmed by it; a future where they are the mindful masters of their digital lives.

Chapter 13: The Role of Policy and Society in Encouraging Digital Detox

Legislative Efforts to Manage Screen Time: Case Studies

As we enter the third decade of the 21st century, our relationship with technology is more complex than ever. The digital devices we interact with daily are not only tools of convenience but also sources of distraction, stress, and, ironically, disconnection. In response to this digital overload, a movement is growing — a movement towards digital detox, a conscious decision to set limits on the use of electronic devices for enhanced wellbeing.

In this chapter, we'll explore how policy and societal norms can encourage and facilitate this shift. We'll discuss various legislative efforts around the world aimed at managing screen time and fostering a healthier relationship with technology.

While we as individuals are the ultimate decision-makers when it comes to our tech usage, it's essential to understand that policy and societal attitudes play a significant role in shaping our behaviors and habits.

The French "Right to Disconnect" Law

First, let's travel to France, a country known for its strong labor laws and a cultural appreciation for work-life balance. In 2017, France passed a law that became a landmark example of legislative efforts towards digital detox. This law, known as the "Right to Disconnect," essentially allows employees to ignore business-related digital communications outside of working hours.

In an age when the boundaries between professional and personal life are increasingly blurred, this policy aims to protect workers from the perils of overconnectivity, such as burnout, stress, and other mental health issues. France's bold step raises important questions about the impact of constant digital communication on our wellbeing and highlights the role of legislation in addressing these issues.

South Korea's Shutdown Law

South Korea, a country at the forefront of digital technology and innovation, has faced its unique set of challenges. One of the most pressing is the high prevalence of internet addiction among young people. In response, the government passed the Shutdown Law, also known as the Cinderella Law, in 2011.

This law mandates that children under 16 are blocked from accessing online gaming sites from midnight until 6 AM. While the law has received mixed reactions and its

effectiveness is still under review, it is an example of a
governmental response to managing screen time and
dealing with the consequences of digital saturation.

Legislative Efforts in Schools

While workplace and gaming regulations are important,
we must not forget the role of education in shaping our
relationship with technology. In many countries, schools
have started implementing their own policies to limit
screen time and encourage healthier tech habits.

In Canada, for example, the Toronto District School Board
banned cell phones in classrooms in 2019, allowing their
use only for educational purposes or to support special
needs. Similarly, the Australian state of Victoria has also
banned mobile phones in all public primary and secondary
schools to minimize distractions and cyberbullying.

On a larger scale, China has implemented stringent
regulations limiting the number of online video games for
minors, as well as their playtime. This bold move is aimed
at curbing video game addiction, improving children's
physical health, and encouraging more traditional forms of
play and study.

Moving Forward

While these case studies provide an overview of how different societies are dealing with the implications of digital saturation, it's important to note that there is no one-size-fits-all solution. Each culture, each society, and indeed, each individual, will have their unique challenges and responses.

However, what these legislative efforts underscore is the urgent need for policies that foster healthier digital behaviors. And even if the laws are imperfect, they at least provoke conversation, raise awareness, and move us closer towards a more mindful, balanced relationship with technology.

The Emergence of Right to Disconnect Laws and Their Impact

The Right to Disconnect Laws, as pioneered by France, are a significant milestone in our approach to work-life balance in the digital age. These laws offer protection to employees from the expectation of being 'always on,' which has been exacerbated by the increased availability and convenience of digital communication tools.

The effects of this constant connectivity on mental health and overall well-being are increasingly well-documented. Overuse of technology can lead to burnout, increased stress levels, anxiety, and a general decline in personal

relationships. The right to disconnect offers a legal remedy
to these issues by re-establishing boundaries between
work and personal life.

The impacts of such laws are manifold. On an individual
level, they provide employees with time to rest, recuperate,
and engage in non-work activities, which in turn can
improve productivity and job satisfaction. On a broader
societal level, these laws stimulate dialogue about the role
of technology in our lives and encourage businesses to
adopt more mindful digital practices.

Moreover, the emergence of these laws has had a ripple
effect worldwide. Countries such as Italy, Spain, and the
Philippines have followed suit, introducing their versions
of the right to disconnect law, recognizing the importance
of separating work and personal time.

Society's Role in Shaping a Mindful Digital Culture

While legislation plays a crucial role in setting boundaries,
the creation of a mindful digital culture also largely
depends on societal attitudes and behaviors. Society,
through its various institutions such as schools, families,
and social circles, can significantly influence how we use
and perceive technology.

For example, parents modeling mindful technology use can influence their children's screen habits. Schools can implement policies that encourage students to engage in face-to-face social interactions and teach them about responsible digital citizenship. Employers can foster work cultures that respect personal time and discourage excessive screen use.

Media and advertising also play a significant role in shaping our digital culture. By promoting responsible tech use and featuring narratives around digital detox, they can influence public perception and behavior.

Lastly, peer influence, especially among younger generations, can't be underestimated. As digital detox becomes more mainstream, and as more people share their positive experiences, it can inspire others to follow suit, gradually changing the societal norms around tech use.

New Directions: The Rise of Tech-free Tourism and Digital Sabbatical Movements

Recognizing the growing need for a break from constant connectivity, new trends like tech-free tourism and digital sabbatical movements have emerged.

Tech-free tourism is a niche yet rapidly growing market within the travel industry. Destinations and accommodations market themselves as 'digital detox retreats,' offering guests a chance to disconnect from their digital devices and reconnect with nature and themselves. These retreats typically offer outdoor activities, wellness programs, and an environment free from Wi-Fi and screens. The popularity of such retreats indicates a growing desire to escape the digital noise and experience life beyond screens.

Digital sabbaticals, on the other hand, refer to taking an extended break from digital devices. This could range from a week to a month or more, depending on an individual's preference and circumstances. These sabbaticals provide an opportunity to reflect on one's relationship with technology, explore non-digital hobbies, and foster deeper, more meaningful connections with others.

The rise of tech-free tourism and digital sabbatical movements is a testament to a growing recognition of the need for balance in our digital lives. It points to a future where mindful technology use is not just a personal choice but a societal norm.

In the end, creating a healthy digital culture involves a concerted effort from individuals, societies, and legislators. While there's still a long way to go, the current trends and initiatives suggest we are moving in the right direction.

Chapter 14: Building Mindful Organizations in the Digital Era

The Costs of Constant Connectivity in the Workplace

In this era of technology, we are relentlessly tethered to our digital devices. The lines between our personal and professional lives have blurred as smartphones, laptops, and smartwatches keep us connected to work emails, reports, and meetings, even outside office hours. But is this constant connectivity beneficial or detrimental to us and the organizations we are part of?

This chapter will unravel the complexities surrounding the notion of constant connectivity, its costs on our work-life balance, health, productivity, and more importantly, how we can transform our digitally overloaded organizations into mindful workplaces. Let's delve into the intriguing world of the digital work era, where the motto is often 'always on, never off.'

The Cost to Our Work-Life Balance

A constant, round-the-clock connection to our workplaces has dramatically affected our work-life balance. With our inboxes buzzing at all hours and Zoom meetings crossing time zones, the demarcation between 'work' and 'home' has become almost non-existent. The result? Burnout, stress, and a compromised personal life.

Though the 'always on' culture may make us feel more productive, multiple studies have proven otherwise. Prolonged work hours often lead to chronic stress, deteriorating mental health, and reduced job satisfaction. Even when we're physically away from the office, the digital tether to our work environment hampers our ability to relax, recharge, and reconnect with our personal lives.

The Cost to Our Health

The health costs of our digital work culture cannot be understated. In an attempt to be 'available' round the clock, we tend to ignore our physical well-being. The stress from extended work hours leads to sleep deprivation, anxiety, depression, and even cardiovascular diseases. Our bodies are not designed to endure constant stress, and the physiological effects can be dire.

And it's not just physical health. Constant connectivity also takes a toll on our mental well-being. The pressure to respond to work emails or messages promptly, even after work hours, creates a state of constant alertness and stress. Over time, this chronic stress can lead to serious mental health problems, including anxiety and depression.

The Cost to Our Productivity

Ironically, while the 'always-on' work culture is often hailed as a productivity booster, it could very well be a productivity killer. A growing body of research suggests that constant connectivity leads to decreased efficiency. It's a paradox, but it makes sense when you think about it.

When we're 'always on,' our minds are constantly jumping from one task to another, creating a state of cognitive overload. This multitasking, far from making us more efficient, actually slows us down. Studies have shown that multitasking can reduce productivity by as much as 40%.

Moreover, the pressure of constant connectivity doesn't allow our brains the downtime they need to consolidate information, form connections, and generate creative ideas. In other words, our hyper-connected work culture could be stifling our creativity and innovation.

Creating Mindful Organizations

Despite the costs of constant connectivity, there is a silver lining. Organizations are becoming aware of these problems and are looking for ways to mitigate them. Creating a mindful organization is about more than just unplugging from technology; it's about creating a culture that values balance, health, and productivity.

Mindful organizations recognize that their employees are not machines; they need time to rest, recharge, and connect with their personal lives. These organizations respect boundaries and discourage the 'always-on' culture.

Building such an organization starts with small, but significant changes: setting communication norms about when to disconnect, providing resources for stress management, encouraging regular breaks, fostering an environment that values quality of work over quantity, and most importantly, leading by example. When leaders respect their own and others' boundaries, it sends a powerful message to the entire organization.

Setting Communication Norms

Setting communication norms is a crucial first step in building mindful organizations. This could mean establishing 'quiet hours' when no work-related communication is expected, or having 'no email weekends'. Some organizations even restrict the sending of work-related emails after business hours. This not only prevents the intrusion of work into personal time but also sends a message that it's okay, even expected, to disconnect.

Providing Resources for Stress Management

The prevalence of stress and mental health issues in the workplace calls for proactive measures. Mindful organizations prioritize mental health by providing resources for stress management. This could be in the form of employee assistance programs, mindfulness workshops, or mental health days off.

In addition, fostering a supportive and understanding culture can go a long way in reducing workplace stress. Encouraging open conversations about mental health and creating a stigma-free environment are important steps towards this.

Encouraging Regular Breaks

Our brains are not wired to work continuously for extended periods. We need regular breaks to recharge and maintain peak performance. Encouraging employees to take short, frequent breaks can significantly boost productivity and reduce burnout.

These breaks could involve a short walk, a mindfulness meditation, or even just stepping away from the screen for a few minutes. The key is to encourage a culture where taking breaks is not seen as slacking off but as an essential part of maintaining productivity and well-being.

Fostering a Culture of Quality over Quantity

In the digital age, it's easy to get caught up in the 'busyness' trap, equating long hours with productivity. However, mindful organizations recognize that it's not about how long you work, but how well.

By fostering a culture that values quality over quantity, organizations can move away from the 'always-on' culture and towards a more sustainable and healthy work model. This could mean focusing on outcomes rather than hours worked, encouraging deep work over multitasking, and celebrating efficiency and effectiveness over sheer input.

Leading by Example

Perhaps the most powerful tool for building a mindful organization is leadership. When leaders model healthy work habits, it sets the tone for the entire organization. This could mean leaders themselves adhering to 'quiet hours', taking regular breaks, openly talking about their own work-life balance challenges, and prioritizing their own well-being.

Leaders who demonstrate that they value balance and well-being inspire their teams to do the same. This not only contributes to a healthier and more productive work environment but also builds trust and respect, essential ingredients for a successful organization.

The costs of constant connectivity are significant, but they are not inevitable. By taking conscious steps towards building mindful organizations, we can harness the benefits of the digital era without falling prey to its pitfalls. It requires a shift in mindset, a re-evaluation of our work culture, and a commitment to balance, well-being, and sustainable productivity. After all, our organizations are as healthy as the individuals within them.

Promoting Digital Detox and Mindful Practices in the Corporate World

As our understanding of the costs of constant connectivity deepens, organizations worldwide are beginning to promote digital detox and mindful practices within their ranks. The benefits of such practices are multifold, ranging from improved mental health to increased productivity and enhanced creativity.

A digital detox refers to a period of time during which an individual refrains from using digital devices. It's a purposeful pause, a conscious stepping away from the 'always-on' culture. In the corporate world, promoting a digital detox can take various forms. For instance, some organizations are establishing 'no tech' zones in their offices, spaces where employees can unwind and disconnect from their digital devices.

Additionally, organizations can introduce policies that limit after-hours work communication, thereby allowing employees to disconnect from work when they are at home. Offering digital detox days or weekends, where employees are encouraged to unplug completely from work, can also be an effective strategy.

Mindful practices, on the other hand, involve bringing focused attention to the present moment, reducing distraction, and increasing awareness. Within the corporate world, these practices can include mindfulness training programs, meditation workshops, and even simple daily rituals like starting meetings with a moment of silence.

Organizations that have incorporated mindful practices report better decision-making, improved focus, and increased employee satisfaction. Moreover, these practices can help employees manage stress, reduce burnout, and enhance their overall well-being. By promoting digital detox and mindful practices, corporations can pave the way for a healthier, more balanced, and more sustainable work culture.

The Future of Work: Embracing Slow Tech and Mindful Productivity

As we forge ahead into the future, the way we work is set to undergo profound changes. One of the emerging trends in this regard is the embrace of slow tech and mindful productivity.

Slow tech refers to the use of technology in a way that respects human well-being, relationships, and the environment. It's about using tech mindfully, rather than mindlessly. In the corporate world, slow tech can translate into various practices. This could mean designing tech-free spaces in the office, encouraging employees to switch off notifications during deep work periods, or limiting the use of digital communication tools during certain hours.

Furthermore, organizations can embrace slow tech by prioritizing meaningful human interaction over digital communication, encouraging face-to-face meetings instead of always defaulting to email or instant messaging. In essence, slow tech is about ensuring that technology serves us, rather than the other way around.

Mindful productivity, on the other hand, is about working efficiently and purposefully, without the constant stress and distractions that often accompany modern work culture. It's about doing more by doing less. It recognizes the value of focus, deep work, and regular rest periods.

As we look towards the future, organizations are likely to adopt flexible work models, respect employees' need for downtime, and focus on the quality of work rather than the quantity. The future of work is not about being 'always-on' but about working in ways that respect our natural rhythms, prioritize our well-being, and ultimately, lead to more fulfilling and productive work lives.

Chapter 15: The Next Steps: Embracing a Mindful Life in a Digital World

Reevaluating Our Relationship with Technology

In the expansive, yet intimate, world of tech-digital reality, the lines between our gadgets and our lives have blurred. Our devices and apps have a profound influence on our experiences, decisions, and habits. But as we venture forth in this "Tech Detox" journey, it's crucial we take a moment to reassess this relationship. Are we slaves to our smartphones, or can we master our machines?

As we're stepping into this final chapter, it's worth reminding ourselves of the central mantra:

Technology should serve us, not vice versa. But how do we strike that balance? Let's delve in and find out.

So, just to re-cap some of the most salient aspects covered in this book:

Rediscovering Intentionality

Before the internet, actions were typically purpose-driven. We got up to change the television channel or walked to the library for information. Today, it's easy to mindlessly scroll through pages of content without a clear intention. To foster a healthier relationship with technology, we need to revisit the notion of intentionality.

Ask yourself why you're reaching for your phone. Is it a necessity, a habit, or an escape? Before opening an app, ask yourself what you hope to achieve. By adopting this reflective habit, you can use technology more purposefully and avoid mindless consumption.

Understanding the Value of Your Attention

Your attention is a valuable resource. Tech companies are aware of this. In fact, they compete fiercely for it. They design their devices and apps to be as engaging as possible, often at the expense of your well-being.

Recognize that every second you spend engaged with a device is a second you're not spending elsewhere. A minute less on social media might mean a minute more with a loved one, a book, or a walk in nature. This shift in perspective can be transformative in reevaluating our tech habits.

Creating Tech-Free Zones and Times

One practical way to detox is by creating tech-free zones and times in your home. This could be the dinner table, your bedroom, or certain hours in the day. The objective is to have dedicated spaces and times for human interaction and personal reflection, free from the distracting buzz of technology.

Establishing tech-free zones and times is not about shunning technology. Instead, it promotes a mindful use of tech that respects our need for undivided attention in certain activities.

Taking Control of Notifications

We've all experienced it. You're deeply engrossed in a conversation, a book, or a moment of tranquility, when suddenly a notification pops up, fracturing your attention. It's crucial to take control of these intrusive alerts.

Turn off non-essential notifications. Prioritize who and what can interrupt your day. This simple act can have a profound impact on your attention span and stress levels, reducing the feeling of being 'on-call' 24/7.

Educating Yourself About Tech's Impact

Knowledge is power. Understanding the impact of technology on our mental and physical health can be a strong motivator for change. For instance, excessive screen time has been linked to sleep disturbances, obesity, and anxiety. Conversely, digital tools can also be used to promote physical activity, mindfulness, and positive connections.

Stay informed about these topics. Seek reliable sources, and use this information to make conscious decisions about your tech habits.

Balancing Digital and Analog Activities

Technology can provide entertainment, information, and connections, but it shouldn't replace offline activities. Make an effort to balance digital and analog activities in your life. Cook a meal instead of ordering take-out, read a physical book instead of a digital one, or engage in face-to-face conversation instead of texting.

The goal is not to completely eliminate digital activities but to restore balance and give your mind a break from the incessant influx of digital information.

Being Mindful of Online Interactions

Our online interactions can significantly influence our well-being. Consider how much time you spend on social media and how it makes you feel. Do you compare your life to others? Do you feel the urge to present a perfect life? Social media can be a double-edged sword, offering connection yet breeding discontent.

Strive for authenticity in your online interactions. Follow accounts that inspire positivity, learn from constructive criticism, and disconnect from toxic online environments when necessary.

Prioritizing Quality Over Quantity

The number of likes, shares, or followers we have online can sometimes seem like a measure of our worth. But it's important to realize that these metrics do not define you.

Instead of getting lost in the numbers game, prioritize quality interactions over quantity. It's better to have meaningful exchanges with a few friends than to be overwhelmed by a horde of followers with whom you have superficial interactions.

Mastering Digital Tools

We often fall into the trap of using technology for the sake of using it. Yet, the true power of technology lies in how it can simplify and enrich our lives. Whether it's a fitness tracker to monitor your health, a meditation app for mindfulness, or a budgeting tool to manage your finances - learn to harness technology to serve your needs.

Stay updated on technological advances and be discerning in choosing what suits your lifestyle. The goal is to become a master of technology, not its servant.

Exploring Tech Alternatives

Finally, remember there are alternatives to technology for virtually everything it provides. Instead of a video call, consider a personal meeting. Instead of texting, consider writing a letter. Instead of an online game, consider a board game.

Exploring these tech alternatives allows us to appreciate different ways of connecting, learning, and relaxing. Moreover, it reinforces our belief that we can control our use of technology, instead of allowing it to control us.

As we navigate our tech-laden world, we need to reevaluate our relationship with technology regularly. It's about learning to adapt and thrive, ensuring that technology aids us without overwhelming our lives. With these strategies, you'll be well on your way to a mindful, balanced, and fulfilled life in the digital age.

Every step you take towards mindful living is a victory, no matter how small. So, be patient with yourself and keep moving forward. The journey to a balanced digital life is a marathon, not a sprint. In the words of Arthur Ashe, "Start where you are. Use what you have. Do what you can." You have the power to reshape your digital destiny.

Envisioning a Future of Mindful Tech Use

As we immerse ourselves in the age of digital interactivity and interconnectivity, envisioning a future of mindful tech use can seem like a daunting task. But, believe it or not, it's a challenge that we can indeed rise to, and our collective actions today will shape the technological landscape of tomorrow.

In this mindful future, technology doesn't control us; instead, it becomes an invaluable tool, helping us navigate our lives efficiently. We harness its immense power to enhance our productivity, to deepen our connections with others, to broaden our horizons, and to lead healthier, more balanced lives.

Imagine a world where our digital devices are designed with our well-being in mind - technology that encourages us to take breaks, respect our sleep schedules, and focus on the task at hand. This is not a distant dream; many tech companies have already started incorporating such features. Google's "Digital Wellbeing" initiative and Apple's "Screen Time" feature are steps in this direction.

Envisioning a future of mindful tech use also involves society as a whole. Education systems need to incorporate digital literacy into their curricula, ensuring that future generations understand the benefits and risks associated with technology. Governments must also play their part, implementing regulations that ensure the ethical use of technology.

However, the future is not just about the macro-level shifts in the tech industry or society. It's also about the micro-changes at the individual level. It's about each of us making conscious choices about how, when, and why we use technology. It's about us setting personal boundaries, nurturing mindful habits, and becoming role models for mindful tech use.

Cultivating Ongoing Mindful Habits: A Lifelong Journey

Cultivating mindful habits around technology is not a one-time event. It's a continuous process, a lifelong journey of learning, adapting, and evolving.

Just as we need to maintain physical hygiene, we also need 'digital hygiene'. Regularly 'cleaning up' our digital spaces can go a long way in promoting mindful tech use. This could include deleting unnecessary apps, unsubscribing from redundant mailing lists, or decluttering our social media feeds.

In our journey towards mindfulness, consistency is key. Start small. You could start by spending five minutes a day without any technology. Gradually, you could extend this

The Next Steps: Embracing a Mindful Life in a Digital
World

period or incorporate additional mindful habits. The idea
is not to make drastic changes that are hard to maintain
but to develop sustainable habits that become a natural
part of our lives.

It's also important to recognize that we're not alone in this
journey. Engaging with a community of people who are
striving for the same goals can provide tremendous
support. Online forums, self-help groups, or even a group
of friends can be your allies in this journey. Share your
struggles, celebrate your victories, and learn from each
other's experiences.

Furthermore, remember that mindfulness is not just about
minimizing technology use; it's about maximizing our
awareness of its impact. It's about questioning our tech
habits, noticing how technology makes us feel, and making
conscious decisions based on these observations.

We must also be patient with ourselves. Change is rarely
linear, and it's normal to face setbacks. However, each
stumble is an opportunity for learning and growth. The key
is to remain committed to our goal and persistently strive
for progress.

Let's remember to celebrate our journey. Every step
towards mindful tech use, no matter how small, is a
triumph. It's a testament to our resilience, our
adaptability, and our commitment to lead balanced,
fulfilling lives in the digital age.

In the grand scheme of things, cultivating ongoing mindful habits is less about the destination and more about the journey. It's about the joy of rediscovering our humanity amid the whirlwind of digital advancements. It's about learning to coexist with technology in harmony, striking a balance that empowers us to leverage the digital world's conveniences while safeguarding our mental peace and wellness.

One crucial aspect of this lifelong journey is adaptability. Technology will continue to evolve, and new challenges and opportunities will arise. Therefore, our mindfulness habits will need to be dynamic. We should be willing to reevaluate our strategies, learn from our experiences, and tweak our approach as necessary.

Adopting a learner's mindset will go a long way in this journey. When we see every experience as an opportunity to learn, we can turn even the most adverse situations into catalysts for growth. For instance, if you notice a spike in your screen time, instead of berating yourself, you can treat it as a wake-up call to revisit your digital habits.

Mindful habits should also encompass the choices we make about the technology we bring into our lives. We should strive to select technology that aligns with our values and contributes positively to our lives. For instance, we might choose a phone with built-in screen time management features or an app that promotes mindfulness.

The Next Steps: Embracing a Mindful Life in a Digital World

Regular reflection is another crucial part of this journey. Set aside time every week or month to reflect on your tech habits. Consider what's working well and what isn't. Are there any new challenges you're facing? Are there new opportunities you could leverage? Reflection allows us to stay aware of our habits, make conscious changes, and feel in control of our relationship with technology.

Cultivating ongoing mindful habits is a journey of compassion. Be kind to yourself in this process. It's okay to have days where you spend more time on technology than planned. It's okay to feel overwhelmed by the pace of technological change. The key is to treat these instances not as failures, but as opportunities to learn and grow.

It's a journey that requires patience, persistence, adaptability, reflection, and above all, compassion. By embracing this journey, we can transform our relationship with technology, using it as a tool to enhance our lives rather than letting it govern us. The journey might be long and challenging, but the rewards - a balanced, mindful, and fulfilling life - are undoubtedly worth it.

Concluding Thoughts: From Tech Detox to Mindful Tech Integration

As we approach the conclusion of this chapter and look back on the journey we've undertaken, it's crucial to note that the ultimate aim is not to purge technology from our lives completely. Indeed, the idea is far from it. In this digital age, technology is integral to nearly every aspect of our lives, from communication and work to entertainment and education. Instead, the goal is to transition from a state of mindless tech consumption to a state of mindful tech integration.

Think of it as a diet. The idea isn't to starve ourselves but to cultivate a healthy eating habit. It's about choosing quality over quantity, purpose over mindlessness, and self-care over self-neglect. Similarly, a tech detox isn't about abstaining from technology indefinitely; it's about resetting our relationship with technology and learning to use it mindfully.

In our journey toward mindful tech integration, it's essential to remember that we're not merely passive consumers of technology. We are active participants, capable of influencing how we engage with technology. Every app we open, every notification we respond to, and every digital boundary we set is a testament to our ability to shape our digital experiences.

The Next Steps: Embracing a Mindful Life in a Digital
World

Mindful tech integration is about creating a harmonious blend of online and offline experiences. It's about using technology to enhance our lives, not detract from them. It's about ensuring that our digital interactions are purposeful, balanced, and conducive to our overall well-being.

As we integrate technology mindfully into our lives, let's be vigilant not to lose sight of what truly matters. Let's not allow our devices to overshadow the importance of face-to-face conversations, the beauty of a quiet moment, or the joy of being fully present in our surroundings.

After all, life isn't happening on our screens; it's happening right here, right now, in the tangible world around us.

Technology in itself is not the enemy. It's a tool, and like any tool, its impact depends on how we use it. Used mindfully, technology can be a powerful ally, opening up a world of knowledge, connecting us with people around the globe, and simplifying complex tasks.

Lastly, mindful tech integration is an ongoing journey, not a destination. It requires continuous effort, learning, and adaptation. But the rewards—a healthier mind, stronger relationships, and a more balanced life—are well worth the effort.

In the grand scheme of things, our journey from tech detox to mindful tech integration is not just about transforming our relationship with technology. It's also about reclaiming our time, our attention, and ultimately, our lives. It's about redefining what productivity, connection, and entertainment mean to us in this digital age.

Most importantly, it's about rediscovering our capacity to live mindfully, joyfully, and fully, both online and offline.

As we conclude this chapter, and indeed, this book, let's carry forward the insights and strategies we've gleaned, applying them not just to our digital lives but to our entire lives.

Here's to a future of mindful tech use, a future where technology serves us, and we're no longer at its mercy. And on that hopeful note, we move forward, armed with newfound knowledge, ready to embrace a life of balance and mindfulness in the digital age.

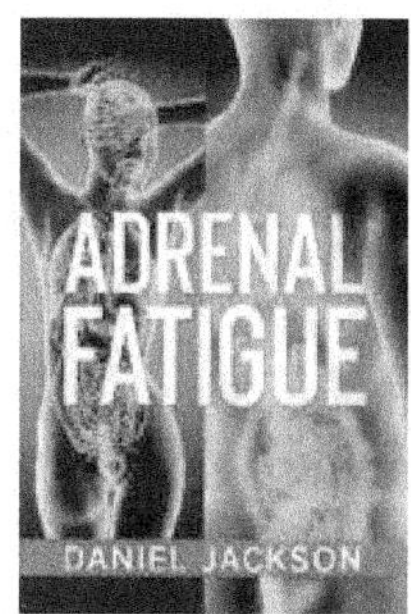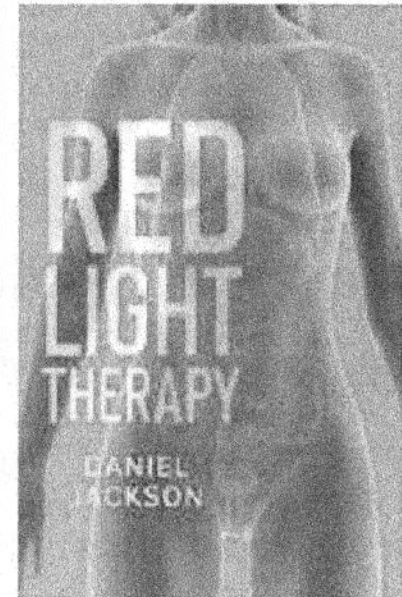

Take a look at more great books available from Rockwood Publishing

... some for FREE!

Just visit the link below:

rockwoodpublishing.co.uk

websites listed in this book. The inclusion of any website links does not necessarily imply a recommendation or endorse the views expressed within them. Rockwood Publishing takes no responsibility for, and will not be liable for, the websites being temporarily unavailable or being removed from the Internet. The accuracy and completeness of information provided herein and opinions stated herein are not guaranteed or warranted to produce any particular results, and the advice and strategies contained herein may not be suitable for every individual. The author shall not be liable for any loss incurred as a consequence of the use and application, directly or indirectly, of any information presented in this work. This publication is designed to provide information in regards to the subject matter covered. The information included in this book has been compiled to give an overview of the subject(s) and detail some of the symptoms, treatments etc. that are available to people with this condition. It is not intended to give medical advice. For a firm diagnosis of your condition, and for a treatment plan suitable for you, you should consult your doctor or consultant. The writer of this book and the publisher are not responsible for any damages or negative consequences following any of the treatments or methods highlighted in this book. Website links are for informational purposes and should not be seen as a personal endorsement; the same applies to the products detailed in this book. The reader should also be aware that although the web links included were correct at the time of writing, they may become out of date in the future.

Disclaimers

The content contained within this book is for information and entertainment purposes only, and in no way purports to represent professional medical opinion. It should NOT be used as a substitute for expert advice, and you must consult with your designated health professional before acting upon any information contained herein or before undertaking any practice whose methodology is referred to in this book. The author is NOT a registered health professional and the text merely represents personal opinion, not medical fact. The author cannot be held responsible for the consequences of any action derived from the reading of this book, as the content is not based on diagnosis and subsequent regimen. It is the reader's responsibility to seek proper, professional medical advice from a registered health practitioner in connection with any material contained within this book.

Legal Disclaimer (part 1)

Nothing in this book should be construed as an attempt to diagnose, treat or cure. The information in this book is intended to be a community resource. The author takes no responsibility for any informational material or brochures produced using information taken from this book. The author has endeavoured to ensure that all information is correct at the time of publication. This information, however, is subject to change without notice. The author makes no warranty with regard to the accuracy of any information and will not be liable for any errors or omissions. Any liability that arises as a result of this information is hereby excluded to the fullest extent allowed by law.

This information should not be used as a substitute for seeking independent professional advice.

Legal Disclaimer (part 2)

Disclaimer and Terms of Use:

a) i. In publishing this information, the author makes no representations concerning the efficacy, appropriateness or suitability of any products or treatments. Use this information at your own risk. The compiler is not a doctor and has no medical background or training.

ii. Statements and information regarding dietary supplements, books and any products mentioned have not been evaluated by any health authority and are not intended to diagnose, treat, cure or prevent any disease or health condition.

b) In view of the possibility of human error, neither the author nor any other party involved in providing this information, warrant that the information contained therein is in every respect accurate or complete and they are not responsible nor liable for any errors or omissions that may be found or for the results obtained from the use of such information. The entire risk as to use of this information is assumed by the user.

c) You are encouraged to consult other sources and confirm the information.

d) The information you access is provided "as is". No warranty, expressed or implied, is given as to the accuracy, completeness or timeliness of any information herein, or for obtaining legal advice. To the fullest extent permissible pursuant to applicable law, neither the author nor any other parties who have been involved in the creation, preparation, printing, or delivering of this information assume responsibility for the completeness, accuracy, timeliness, errors or omissions of said information and assume no liability for any direct, incidental, consequential, indirect, or punitive damages as well as any circumstance for any complication, injuries, side effects or other medical accidents to person or property arising from or in connection with the use or reliance upon any information contained herein.

e) The author is not responsible for the contents of any linked site or any link contained in a linked site, or any changes or update to such sites. The inclusion of any link does not imply endorsement by the author. The author makes no representations or claims as to the quality, content and accuracy of the information, services, products, messages which may be provided by such resources, and specifically disclaims any warranties, including but not limited to implied or express warranties of merchantability or fitness for any particular usage, application or purpose.

f) The information provided is general in nature and is intended for educational and informational purposes only. It is not intended to replace or substitute the evaluation, judgment, diagnosis, and medical or preventative care of a physician, paediatrician, therapist and/or health care provider.

g) Any medical, nutritional, dietetic, therapeutic or other decisions, dosages, treatments or drug regimes should be made in consultation with a health care practitioner. Do not discontinue treatment or medication without first consulting your physician, clinician or therapist.

h) By reading this information, you signify your assent to these terms and conditions of use. If you do not agree to these terms and conditions of use, do not read/use this information. If any provision of these terms and conditions of use shall be determined to be unlawful, void or for any reason unenforceable, then that provision shall be deemed severable from this agreement and shall not affect the validity and enforceability of any remaining provisions.

i) The information, services, products, messages and other materials, individually and collectively, are provided with the understanding that the author is not engaged in rendering medical advice or recommendations.

j) The information and the terms of use are subject to change without notice. The material provided as is without warranty of any kind and may include inaccuracies and/or typographical errors. The author makes no representations about the suitability of this information for any purpose. The author disclaims all warranties with regard to this information, including all implied warranties, and in no event shall the author be held liable, resulting from, or in any way related to, the use of this information.

k) The unauthorized alteration of the content of this information is expressly prohibited. The author, its agents and representatives shall not be responsible for any claims, actions or damages which may arise on account of the unauthorized alteration of this information.